ANCIENT SPELLCRAFT

From the Hymns of the Hittites
to the Carvings of the Celts

By
Laura Perry

NEW PAGE BOOKS
A Division of Career Press, Inc.
Franklin Lakes, NJ

Copyright © 2002 by Laura Perry

All rights reserved under the Pan-American and International Copyright Conventions. This book may not be reproduced, in whole or in part, in any form or by any means electronic or mechanical, including photocopying, recording, or by any information storage and retrieval system now known or hereafter invented, without written permission from the publisher, The Career Press.

Ancient Spellcraft
Edited and Typeset by Kristen Mohn
Cover design by Diane Y. Chin
Printed in the U.S.A. by Book-mart Press

To order this title, please call toll-free 1-800-CAREER-1 (NJ and Canada: 201-848-0310) to order using VISA or Master Card, or for further information on books from Career Press.

The Career Press, Inc., 3 Tice Road, PO Box 687,
Franklin Lakes, NJ 07417
www.careerpress.com
www.newpagebooks.com

Library of Congress Cataloging-in-Publication Data

Perry, Laura, 1965-
　Ancient spellcraft : from the hymns of the Hittites to the carvings of the Celts / by Laura Perry.
　　p. cm.
　Includes bibliographical references and index.
　ISBN 1-56414-576-X (pbk.)
　　1. Magic, Ancient. I. Title.

BF1591 .P47 2001
133.4'4—dc21

2001044266

Dedication

To Awahili, who believed in me.

Acknowledgments

I have worked long and hard to bring this book to print, but I would not have succeeded without the help of some very special people. First, I must thank Trish Telesco for putting me in contact with New Page Books and helping me through the proposal process. Her literary advice and writer's workshops have proved invaluable. I highly recommend her workshops to anyone who wishes to write professionally in any field. I also owe a debt of thanks to the editors at New Page Books for putting up with my incessant questions and patiently providing answers and assistance. My DragonTree Grove and Keltoi Tribe family has given me moral support and much love over the course of my writing career, encouraging me to continue when I wanted to give in and give up. I hope they know how much I appreciate their presence in my life. And finally, I must thank my husband for his kind and patient support as I plunged headlong into a writer's life.

To these people I owe thanks. Of course, any errors or omissions remain my own.

Contents

Introduction	9
Chapter 1 Casting a Spell	13
Chapter 2 The Ancient World	35
Chapter 3 Prosperity	53
Chapter 4 Romance	83
Chapter 5 Fertility	105

CHAPTER 6 Protection	133
CHAPTER 7 Healing	169
CHAPTER 8 Divination	195
Bibliography	215
Index	219
About the Author	224

Introduction

The ancient world is a magickal place. From the groves of the Celts, the temples of Crete, and the pyramids of Egypt, the ancients call to us. "Let our magick live on in you!" they say. For magick never dies, but only slumbers, awaiting discovery by those who would once again revel in its beauty and respect its power.

Come along on a journey through the magickal ancient world. Explore the mysteries of a host of civilizations that echo from our distant past. Within these pages you will find spells and charms from the haunting ancient cultures of Europe, the Mediterranean, and the Middle East.

The people of these mighty ancient civilizations saw themselves as servants to the gods. They believed that if they served their gods well, the gods would reward them. In exchange for the people's service, the gods protected them from illness and bad luck. These ancient peoples also requested aid from their gods through spells and offerings, and received information through dreams and divination. The same goddesses and gods who offered their blessings to the people of the ancient world still offer these gifts to us today.

This is a practical book of spells and charms derived from a number of ancient pagan cultures including the Babylonians, Canaanites, Celts, Cretans, Egyptians, Etruscans, Hittites, Phoenicians, and Sumerians. These cultures fascinate the modern world with their mysterious ruins and enigmatic inscriptions. But more to the point, these ancient civilizations provide a wealth of magickal workings—spells, charms, and divinations—that are simple and practical for modern use.

The six sections of the book speak to the many human needs and desires of prosperity, romance, fertility, healing, protection, and divination of the future. Each section begins with a brief, straightforward discussion of the ways in which these ancient cultures called on their deities for aid in each particular aspect of life. This brief discussion is immediately followed by a host of practical, easy-to-do spells and charms gleaned from the texts and archaeological evidence of these fascinating ancient cultures.

Each spell is described in detail, complete with backgrounds of the deities involved as well as step-by-step instructions for completing the magickal working. The spells are clear and precise enough to put beginners and historical dabblers at ease, but also provide enough background information to satisfy those more experienced with magickal workings. The spells and charms are all designed with a positive outcome in mind, heeding always the admonition to do no harm to oneself or others.

As you journey through these pages and into the magick of the ages, you will find spells and charms of all sorts.

Introduction

Refer to them frequently as you find the need for prosperity of your purse and your life; romance and love; fertility for you, your garden, and your pets; healing of all sorts; protection from misfortune; and divination of the future. Read them for their historical interest and fascination. But above all, make them a very real part of your magickal life every day.

Chapter 1

 Casting A Spell

spell: n. *"a spoken word or form of words held to have magic power: INCANTATION"* (Webster's New Collegiate Dictionary, *1109)*

What a powerful image can be invoked with the three simple words: casting a spell. Images of the ancient priest in his temple darkened by incense smoke, the medieval witch dancing around her cauldron, and the modern pagan priestess wielding her athame as she casts a circle drift through our minds. For age upon age, since long before people began writing down their history, we have turned to deities and natural forces to help us shape our lives the way we want them to be. This is the legacy of these ancient peoples, a valuable bequest to those of us in the modern world who are willing to listen and learn.

For a time, much of the information about spellcasting and magick was lost, fallen into disuse, or hidden in fear. But now it has come back to help us build more fulfilling lives and rekindle the knowledge of our true place in the universe. As we relearn the value of magick and respect its place in our lives, we can turn to a long history of its use in many cultures around the world. We can learn from them,

Ancient Spellcraft

and as we learn, we shed a little more light on the realm of spellwork. It is exciting indeed, but it need not be so mysterious. In the chapters that follow, you will discover just how easy it is to tap into this ancient source of power to bring goodness into your life.

When we talk about this kind of magick, we say we are casting a spell. It is a common phrase, but what does it really mean? What power do these three simple words really have? Spelling (casting spells) is a very special kind of magick; simple, yet powerful. A spell is a short, practical ritual with a specific purpose. Spells can shift the energy around us and help us mold our lives to our desires without harming others. Spellcraft (the practice of casting spells) works on a simple principle that all ancient cultures held in common. They believed that focused thought moves energy and brings about the fulfillment of a spell's purpose. When casting a spell, you focus your attention on the desired outcome. Your mind is the muscle that moves the energy. The objects you use and the words you speak are your tools, but words in particular are very powerful tools for spellcasting.

Think about the times in your life when words have had power over you. Remember a time when someone said something that made you happy, sad, angry, or jealous. You had no control over that feeling, did you? Those words had a powerful effect on you, and those aren't even examples of magick, just ordinary speech. If ordinary speech can have such a tremendous effect on you, just think what words can do when used with magickal intent—that's what happens in a spell.

Words have power. The words we use in spells have special power. Because of the commanding effect words can have, I have included the etymologies (word histories) of the subjects that make up the chapters of this book. These words—spell, prosperity, romance, protection, fertility, healing, and divination—all come from ancient roots and have great power. Knowing the histories and roots of these words helps us understand their power and their effect on us. Once we understand the power of words, we can use them more effectively in respectful spellcasting.

First of all, we know that the word *spell* comes from an Indo-European root (*spel-*) that means 'to say aloud or recite,' just as children do today in a spelling bee. Indo-European is the ancient ancestor of most of the modern European languages including English, French, Spanish, Italian, and Russian, among others. The Indo-European roots of our words stretch far back in time, before the age of written history. These roots have gathered strength and meaning over eons, giving great power to the words we speak today.

Ancient Spellcraft

In addition to having a historic root that refers to speech, the word *spell* is related to the familiar word *gospel*, which means "God's sayings" (Watkins, 63). It is also kindred to the Old High German word *spel*, which means speech, story, or tale. From this Old High German word we also get the modern German/Yiddish *spiel*, which has made its way into English slang as a term for a sales pitch. Our modern word *spell* is also related to the Greek word for boasting, *apeile*. In other words, a spell is all about things we say out loud. Spells take their power from words as well as actions.

As you read at the beginning of this chapter, the dictionary definition of a spell equates it with an incantation. Incantation is a familiar word that we toss around with ease, but stop for a moment and think about what it really means. *Incantation* and *enchant* both come from the Latin root *incantare*. This Latin term literally means to "en-chant" something, in other words, to chant or sing until someone or something is under the influence of magick. An incantation, then, is "a written or recited formula of words designed to produce a particular effect" (*Webster's*, 574). Once again, we have the spoken word used as a method of producing a desired effect. Very useful, wouldn't you say? This is part of the power of words, and the power of spells.

Of course, it's not just the spoken word that gives spells their power; the written word is equally powerful. In fact, much of what we know about ancient spellcraft comes from magickal writings and inscriptions made by people in ancient civilizations. The power of the written word shows up in mythology, too. According to ancient Roman mythology, the goddess Carmenta invented the alphabet and, hence, the written words of power. It is from Her name that we get the English word *charm*, which is often used interchangeably with the word *spell*.

Casting a spell—these three simple words form the title of this chapter, but you must not take them at face value. When you say that you cast a spell, "casting" in this case does not mean throwing something, as in the way you might cast a stone across the surface of a pond. In this case, casting means molding something to the shape you desire using your energy, your focus, and your will. When you cast the spells in this book, you will use words, either written or spoken, to formulate and enact your will. Pay careful attention to the words. Don't change them in vehemence or vengeance to seek more than the spell offers or to do harm to others. You may indeed harm others, which of course is not a good thing, and you'll likely harm yourself as well, karma being what it is. The point of spellcraft is to improve your own life, not to make other people's lives worse. Words, and spells, are powerful forces. Always use them with respect.

Some of the spells in the following chapters include sections in which you have to formulate your thoughts into words and then either write the words down or say them aloud. Take the time to find the right words and be sure your words say what is in your heart. Don't rush through just to get the spell finished. It is easy to hurry, tempted by the thought of receiving the spell's promise that much sooner. But take your time. Choose your words very carefully, for the universe can be quite literal. Compose your words before you perform the spell. Set them aside for a while, then look at them again. Be very sure of what you want to say.

The point of casting a spell is to ask for something and then to receive it as a consequence of the spell's magick.

Ancient Spellcraft

The spells in this book will help you ask for things you want and need—prosperity, romance, protection, healing, and so forth. But you must never use these spells at the expense of others. We all have a right to fulfilled lives. We all have a right to ask for the things we want and need. But please be justly desirous, not greedy. The purpose of these spells is to bring good things into your life, not to offer you a tool for outcompeting your neighbor or taking revenge on your boss.

It's a good idea to "check your conscience" about what you intend to do before casting a spell. Make sure the spell is really something you're comfortable doing. Make sure, too, that you're comfortable asking for what the spell offers. Is the result that the spell promises really something you want to add to your life? Consider the mindset of a child who wants something—know what you want and don't doubt for a moment that you deserve it. But be sure you're doing it for your own happiness, not to fulfill someone else's desires or to create an effect on another person. The only life you have a right to change is your own.

The point of asking for prosperity, romance, and all the rest through spellwork, or any other means for that matter, is to be happy. Think about that as you plan to perform your spell. Will receiving the bounty of the spell's effects make you happy? Reflect on your values and desires before you launch into spellwork. Make sure you're not just trying to fill up empty space in your life that would be better filled with community service, a more meaningful job, or a more powerful spiritual experience.

Many ancient spells were long, complicated rituals that had to be performed at a deity's temple, perhaps on a certain day or at a certain time. These days, that level of complexity remains only within the realm of the ceremonial magician. Few of us have the means to travel to the temples of the various deities, even if they are still standing. And few of us have such flexible schedules that we can afford to take time off from work, or get up in the middle of the night, to perform a highly ceremonial spell at its appointed time. Fortunately, simplified versions of the ancient spells are easy to perform wherever we might be, using supplies and equipment that are easy to find in the modern world. And these spells still work very effectively. They still call on the most ancient, holy, and powerful forces in the cosmos.

MEET THE DEITIES

As you read through the spells in this book, you will find that many deities share similar attributes. You will also find that some deities were powerful at one time, then fell into disregard as others rose to power. In ancient times, just as much as today, theology and politics intertwined. The people in power decided which deities were important, which ones the people should worship, and which ones they should ignore. Goddesses and gods changed names and attributes over time as cultures clashed, divided, and blended. The ancient civilizations whose spells fill this book had a great deal of contact with each other. Around the Mediterranean, throughout the Middle East, and across Europe they traded with each other, sharing culture and religion along with consumer goods. As the cultures mingled and shifted, their deities either rose in prominence or sank into obscurity. So if you begin to feel that many of the deities are

Ancient Spellcraft

closely related, or are perhaps even renamed versions of each other, you are indeed correct. Such is the way of the spiritual world.

Each spell within these pages gives a glimpse of the culture it is derived from, a snapshot in time, pure and simple. The deities each spell calls on had their heyday in their own culture, among the people who gave them a home in the temples and shrines of that particular civilization. Over time, some of the powerful goddesses and gods of these ancient civilizations shifted into the background as new deities rose in popularity. Sometimes the Goddess in Her many guises held sway throughout the land, and sometimes the God ruled over the other deities. Though their place within these ancient traditions changed over time, each deity whose name appears in these spells still carries power and magick and still deserves the utmost respect.

You will find more goddesses than gods in these spells because that's the way most of these ancient civilizations were oriented. Throughout the Mediterranean basin and the Middle East especially, the Goddess reigned supreme over vast cultures for millennia. We now realize that the deities of any given society reflect the cultural norms of that society. Goddesses and gods have always lived, worked, and played in much the same way their people have. Among the civilizations represented in the spells that follow, some were matriarchal, some were equalitarian, and a few were patriarchal. This gives us a total of more dominant female than male deities, though all the deities you will meet in these pages held a place of prominence and respect in their homeland at one time or another. Choose whichever ones speak to you. Remember, there is both feminine and masculine energies in each of us.

One major difference between our modern world and the world of the ancients is the place of religion in people's lives. The great ancient civilizations had no concept of the separation of church and state. For the people in these ancient societies, religion was an integral part of politics and business, as well as daily life. The temples and the priesthood played an active role in the economics and politics of the societies they served. So the people in these ancient cultures saw nothing odd about using magick and calling on their deities to create change in every aspect of their lives. They did not wonder whether they should call on a deity for success in business; they only wondered which deity they should choose!

Of course, there are some inherent difficulties with reconstructing any aspect of the past. We must work from archaeological evidence such as temple sites, ritual tools, altars, artwork, and inscriptions. There are often gaps in the information available to us in spite of the diligent work done by archaeologists and historians. The ancient written texts we have are often biased according to the authors' religious and political ideologies. Consequently, we have to fill in the gaps in this information, sometimes making educated guesses based on the available evidence. It is these educated guesses that cause disagreement among those interested in ancient cultures. In the spells that follow, I have relied on archaeological evidence and generally accepted historical reconstruction. My point here is not to insist that any one perspective is the only correct one, but rather to use all the available information to provide you with culturally accurate rituals that are simple and practical to perform.

Ancient Spellcraft

If you are interested in the history and archaeology of any of the ancient civilizations represented in these spells, by all means, turn to the books listed in the bibliography. There is a great deal of fascinating information available about the civilizations that fill our past. The more we know about them, the better we can connect with their spirituality.

Proper manners for safety

Ancient cultures have bequeathed us not only a host of haunting ruins—temples, forts, and long-abandoned cities—but also a legacy of magick that calls on the deities that humanity has worshiped for age upon age. This magick is real and it is powerful. Please do not use these spells in jest or in play. Respect yourself, those around you, and above all, the gods whose energy powers the magick.

Many of these spells include prayers to the deities who are called on within the spell. Please be aware that the term 'to pray' comes from a root that means 'to beg.' While you may not be on your knees groveling before the gods in these spells, please bear in mind that you are asking a favor of an entity far more powerful than you. An ancient Egyptian prayer says, "all good fates lie in the hands of the gods." Always address the deities with respect and always give thanks for what you receive through spellwork. Being ungrateful is both rude and dangerous. One of the oldest hymns known to mankind was written by a Babylonian leader in thanks to the Sun/Creator god Marduk for victory in war. The leader had asked Marduk for victory beforehand and thanked the generous giver afterwards. Now that's good manners—the kind that is likely to make Marduk do you a favor again sometime.

Speaking of manners, be careful what you ask for—you just may get it! Be sure you really want what the spell promises to produce for you. Read through the whole spell beforehand and make sure it is something you really want to do. Don't hurry or rush through any of these spells. Perform them with patience and respect. And never, never perform any spell in jest. To do so is to invoke the wrath of the deities you insult.

Of course, don't go and do anything nasty to other people. That's not what these spells are for, so please don't make changes in them that might cause harm to others. What goes around comes around, and you aren't doing anyone a favor by trying to harm someone. Protection spells are just that—protection. They keep harm from coming to you, but they don't do harm to others. Please keep it that way. Thank you.

A number of the spells in the following chapters have you dispose of an item in a body of water or in the earth, or have you collect water or earth from a natural source. Please use caution and respect land ownership in these instances. Please don't trespass and don't take rocks, dirt, or plant matter from state and national parks (that's illegal). If you want to use someone's land to perform a spell, be sure to get their permission first. It's bad karma to do a wrong to someone in order to perform part of a spell, and that includes trespassing. At the least, your spell won't work and at the most, you may find your life going to pot for such acts. There are plenty of people who are happy to have earth-revering types use their land, so seek them out and work your spells with a clear conscience.

Some of the spells in this book direct you to dispose of items used in the spell in certain ways. If you intend to bury a magickal item or throw it into a body of water, again, please be considerate and get the landowner's permission first. Once you have completed your spell, you may find that you have food or ritual items left over. Please do not dispose of these things casually. They have been used for magick and are no longer ordinary objects. Instead of wasting food, share it with others or add it to your compost. It is perfectly acceptable to eat and drink the leftovers from a spell. Just be sure not to consume any portion you have given to a deity. Other disposable items—parchment, string, and so forth—can be used again or buried. Please don't just throw them in the trash. Non-disposable objects such as bowls and jars, of course, can simply be reverently returned to their regular use.

THE TRUE MEANING OF SACRIFICE

A sacrifice requires giving up something meaningful, usually in exchange for something of value. Most ancient societies practiced sacrifice of various sorts as part of their regular worship. This included human and animal sacrifice as well as the giving of valuable items such as wine, incense, and jewelry to the gods. Ancient people believed that offering such sacrifices to their deities would ensure that the deities acted favorably toward them. After all, aren't you more likely to go out of your way for someone who has showered you with gifts?

In the case of the spells in this book, the sacrifice is made to the deity invoked in the spell. You give the sacrifice in exchange for the deity's aid in working the spell. The point of sacrifice is that whatever you give up has value to you, so that the giving up of it is a loss to you. Long ago, ancient peoples gave up to their deities the thing they valued the most—life itself. The sacrifice of a living being is no longer acceptable, but sacrifice in other forms is still a powerful part of spellcasting.

Many of these spells direct you to make an offering or sacrifice of some sort—a gift to the deity you are calling on. The more a sacrificial item means to you, the more powerful the working that it engenders will be. For instance, if you're going to offer incense to a deity as part of a spell, make it your best incense, not the stuff you want to get rid of. Give your best whiskey, your favorite earrings, and so forth. If you don't care that the item is gone, then it wasn't a sacrifice and will not empower the spell.

Methods of spellcasting

A spell is essentially a miniature ritual with a very practical purpose. It includes all the basic elements of ritual—denoting the space in which the rite will be performed, calling on the deity, praising the deity, asking for favors, and formally closing the ritual (usually with thanks and more praise). Incidentally, with the exception of denoting the sacred space, this is the same format that prayer takes. In fact, many ancient prayers are simple spells, calling on a deity for favors of various sorts in return for praise or the promise of certain actions or behaviors.

Spells have taken many different forms throughout history. For instance, the Romans popularized a kind of spell called a *votum*. The word literally means 'a vow.' But rather

Ancient Spellcraft

than a typical vow with another human being, a *votum* was a deal with a deity. In other words, the person performing the *votum* told the deity, "I'll do x if you'll give me y." We often do this in modern life in a less formal way, sometimes without realizing it. Perhaps you have caught yourself thinking to your favorite deity, "If you give us beautiful weather on the day of the event, I'll work at the soup kitchen for three weekends in a row." The only real difference is that the ancient *votum* formalized the deal so the Romans didn't dare back out of their promise.

Repetition is a common component of spellcasting. It helps to put you into a meditative or trance-like mindset, allowing your powerful subconscious mind to aid you in your magickal workings. Reciting a repetitive chant while counting the repetitions on a knotted string dates back to at least 500 B.C.E. with Indic priests in the Middle East. Repetition impresses on your mind the subject that you are repeating and increases the effectiveness of your spell.

Many ancient traditions required certain numbers of repetitions of chants or prayers. Sometimes the repetitions numbered in the tens or hundreds so it would be easy to lose track if you tried to count in your head. As a memory aid, many of these people used knotted strings, one knot for each repetition. They simply moved their hand down the knotted string with each repetition without having to worry about counting. You can also use small items strung on a cord or ribbon for the same purpose. Beads, nuts, cherry pits, and small bones work well. In fact, such strings of beads form the origin of the Catholic and Buddhist rosaries.

Some spells take repetition to a higher level, requiring the entire spell to be repeated on successive nights. The ancient Greeks performed a spell called a *novena*, from the Greek word for the number nine. The *novena* required repeating the whole spell for nine days in a row. The number nine has long been sacred to many cultures, as has the number three. Many spells require triple repetitions of chants or actions, for emphasis and power. Often the number of repetitions in a spell is keyed to the number that is sacred to the deity whom the spell calls on.

The practical nitty-gritty

Each spell in the following chapters includes a list of supplies you will need as well as detailed instructions for performing the spell—a magickal "recipe" for each spell, complete with ingredients and cooking directions. Please take the time to read the whole spell through, make sure it's what you really want to do, and collect all your supplies beforehand so you can perform the spell uninterrupted. Don't get up in the middle of a spell to search for something you forgot! Make sure you have gathered all of the necessary components so you can concentrate on the spell rather than worrying about your supplies. You will need to clear your mind and remove distractions before beginning any spellwork. This may mean sending the kids outside to play, turning off the TV, or going out under your favorite tree to be alone. Always quiet your mind and concentrate on the purpose of your spell before you begin.

Sacred Space For Spells

Unlike performing a ritual, you are not required to formally mark sacred space before performing these spells,

Ancient Spellcraft

but doing so can help with the power of the spell. From a cosmic perspective, all space is sacred. But our puny human minds simply can't contemplate all space at once, so we mark out a small section of it to focus on as sacred while we do our rituals. The ancients performed spells in temples, groves, and other places that had visible boundaries so they didn't need to cast a circle or anything similar. If you have a special place you go to do rituals, you may not need to mark the sacred space before you begin. But if you're working in your backyard, in the living room, or even in the kitchen, stop and use your favorite method of marking sacred space beforehand so you can concentrate better on what you're doing. At the very least, look around you and mentally note the physical boundaries of your space—the walls of a room, the fence around your backyard, or the trees that surround a park or field.

The psychology of ritual and spellwork says that set and setting are powerful influences. In other words, if you feel like you're in a special place, then your concentration will improve and the energy of the spell will be more powerful. So it's worth it to set up your surroundings with some care and choose props that make you feel magickal. The more magickal your surroundings feel to you, the more impact your spell will have. And you don't necessarily have to use props and accessories to achieve that magickal feeling. Perhaps there is a place in nature that feels magickal to you—deep in the woods, or beside a waterfall, or on top of a hill. Whatever speaks to you, whether it is carefully chosen props, a special outfit, or a certain spot outdoors, that is what will put you in the right frame of mind to perform powerful spells.

And of course, in a pinch, practicality works, too. If you feel the pressing need to perform a spell, but you don't have the supplies for a complicated setup, you can still perform an effective spell. Use the materials you have available, as long as they fit within the basic requirements of the spell. Just be sure to spend plenty of time quieting your mind before you begin and make an extra effort to concentrate on the purpose of the spell as you do the magickal working. This will assure you the best results even if you don't have the fanciest setup around.

The Magickal Mindset

When you perform these spells, regardless of how elaborate your setup is, be sure to take some time to clear your mind and perhaps meditate a bit in advance. Set aside the concerns of daily life and concentrate on the spell you will be doing. The more fully you focus on the spell, the stronger its impact will be.

When you're doing these spells, focus and concentrate on the end result, not on how you're going to get there. The universe takes the path of least resistance, the shortest and most efficient route to your goal, and it may not be what you expect. So don't tell the universe how to get there—you may limit your possibilities. You may not actually know what the best way is to achieve your goal and you may be surprised by how it finally happens. Just let it happen. Don't have any expectations except that somehow, like magick, it will indeed occur.

Gathering Your Supplies

In terms of the drinks used in these spells, nonalcoholic beverages are always an acceptable substitute where wine or

Ancient Spellcraft

other alcoholic beverages are mentioned. White or purple grape juice makes a good visual substitute for white or red wine. It often sounds to us like the ancients drank an enormous amount of wine, but most ancient peoples actually considered wine too powerful to drink undiluted. They mixed their wine with water, often diluting it down considerably before drinking it. They considered drunkenness to be rude and uncivilized, definitely not socially acceptable. So don't worry that your spell will fail because you prefer not to drink alcohol, simply substitute a similar nonalcoholic beverage and perform your spell with confidence.

When a spell calls for parchment on which to write words or draw symbols, this means antique-style parchment-looking paper. Real parchment (vellum) is made from lambskin or calfskin, and you're not likely to find it at your local office supply store. Plain white paper will do in a pinch but parchment-style paper is more ambient. As I noted earlier, the props you choose can make your spell even more powerful, so take the time to peruse your local store for paper that looks like antique parchment. It's available fairly readily and can make a big difference in how you feel about your spell.

The detailed instructions for each spell include a list of supplies and a set of instructions for actually performing the spell. This includes all the actions you need to perform and the words you need to say in order to complete the spell. The parts you must say out loud are always enclosed in quotation marks. Sometimes the spoken segments need to be repeated. If this is the case, the instructions will note how many repetitions you need to complete. Simply follow the directions and you will soon be casting spells with ease.

This may seem like a lot of information, but most of it is really just common sense. Let your conscience be your guide and enjoy your journey through the fascinating world of ancient spellcraft.

CHAPTER 2

The Ancient World

The civilizations referred to in these spells cannot be found on any modern map. Even the ancient Greek Empire stretched far beyond the boundaries of the modern nation of Greece. Let's review the ancient civilizations represented within these pages, including their geographic locations and the names of the deities they worshiped. Once you become familiar with the different civilizations and their deities, you will be able to connect more easily with their magick. Though they are far removed from us in time, the people of these ancient cultures had desires and needs very much like our own. They had families and jobs, and they wished for prosperity, romance, fertility, protection, and healing, just as we do. Their world is also our world, a little farther down the path of time.

Don't be surprised if you see several of the ancient civilizations described below as occupying the same area. These ancient nations and empires spanned several millennia and some of them succeeded others in the same geographic territory.

Ancient Spellcraft

Many of these civilizations overlapped and intertwined both politically and geographically. But we give them distinct names and defined borders in order to study them with less confusion. Think of it this way: There was already a distinct American culture in the British Colonies in North America long before the United States officially became a separate country in 1776. So while the area was still officially a British colony, we can also think of it as an American civilization. In much the same way, the ancient civilizations represented in these chapters are defined culturally, since many of them overlapped or were adjacent in geographic and political terms.

In fact, many of these ancient civilizations were ethnically mixed due to the shifting of political boundaries. For instance, the Phoenician Empire grew out of the Canaanite settlements at the coastal cities of Tyre and Sidon in modern-day Palestine. But the Phoenicians had a unique culture and society that was distinct from that of their Canaanite predecessors. So when we talk about the Phoenicians, we are referring to a culture in a specific geographic area at a certain time in history.

The civilizations of the ancient world varied greatly in a number of different regards. They had different industries and trades, different customs and clothing, and different food. But these empires all had one thing in common—they revered the divine in the form of the Goddess and the God, asking Them for favors through many different kinds of spells and rites.

Don't worry. It isn't nearly as complicated as it sounds. In order to get your bearings, refer to the map as you read about the cultures you encounter in the spells that follow.

The Ancient World

Please note that I use the currently accepted terms B.C.E. and C.E. rather than the outmoded (and Christian-based) terms B.C. and A.D. in reference to dates. B.C.E. means "Before Common Era" and corresponds to the obsolete term B.C. C.E. simply means "Common Era" and corresponds to A.D. Historians now use the terms B.C.E. and C.E. in order to refer to dates without cloaking their data in a Christian aura, because history includes all religions, not just one.

Please bear in mind that most of the deity names listed in these spells were originally written not only in other languages, but in other alphabets as well, and many of them in hieroglyphics or cuneiform. Because the civilizations that worshiped these gods and goddesses have long since disappeared, we have to rely on archaeological evidence for their names and attributes, as well as for the customs surrounding their worship. Within these pages you will find spellings commonly accepted by the archaeologists and scholars who study these civilizations. All deity names are capitalized. The words "god" and "goddess" are capitalized when they are used as the name of a deity, but not just in reference to the concept of deity. Deity pronouns (he, she, him, her) are capitalized out of respect.

Ancient Spellcraft

Ancient Empires

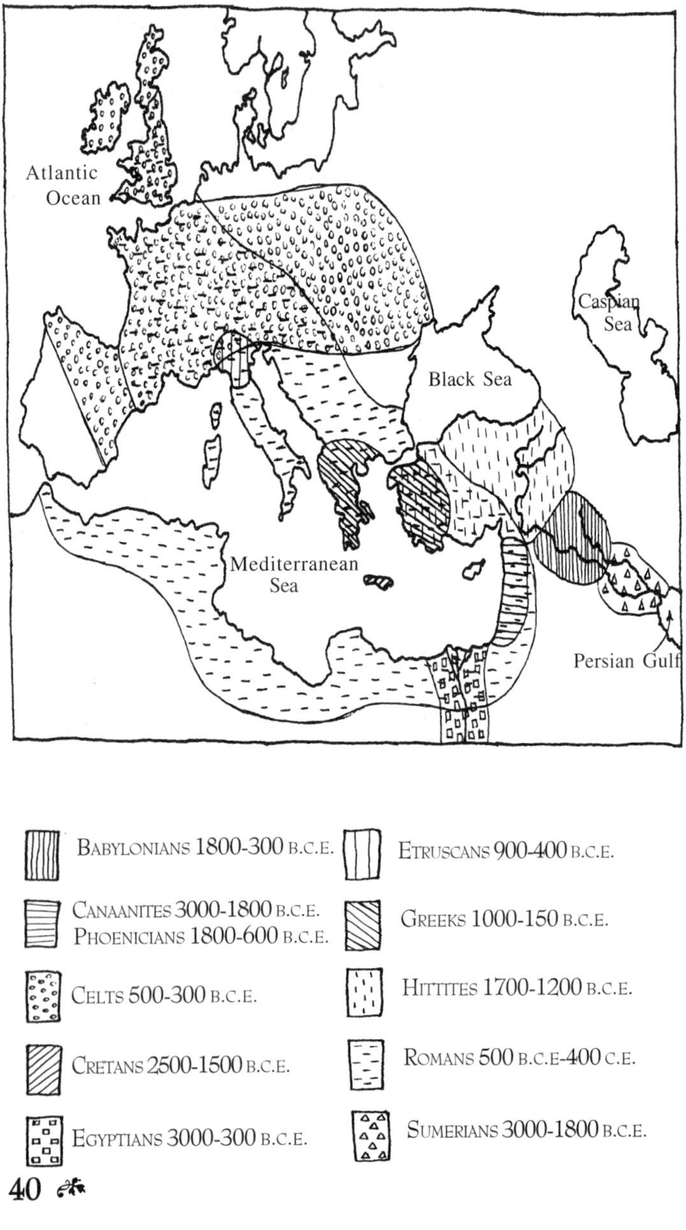

▌	BABYLONIANS 1800-300 B.C.E.	▐	ETRUSCANS 900-400 B.C.E.
▬	CANAANITES 3000-1800 B.C.E. PHOENICIANS 1800-600 B.C.E.	◩	GREEKS 1000-150 B.C.E.
░	CELTS 500-300 B.C.E.	┊	HITTITES 1700-1200 B.C.E.
▨	CRETANS 2500-1500 B.C.E.	─	ROMANS 500 B.C.E-400 C.E.
▥	EGYPTIANS 3000-300 B.C.E.	△	SUMERIANS 3000-1800 B.C.E.

40

BABYLONIANS

Also referred to as the Assyro-Babylonian Empire, this culture flourished in the Middle East from about 1800 to 300 B.C.E. The Babylonians lived in the area called Mesopotamia, also referred to as the Fertile Crescent. Mesopotamia is the region in the Middle East bordered by the Tigris River in the east and Euphrates River in the west. This area is largely within the borders of modern Iraq. The Babylonian Empire encompassed the northern portion of Mesopotamia, including the area around the modern Iraqi city of Baghdad. The ancient Babylonian cities of Babylon, Kish, and Nippur are now hidden beneath the drifting desert sands.

Then as now, this area was a vast desert. The Babylonians and others who lived around the Tigris and Euphrates Rivers had to rely on a complex system of canals to irrigate their croplands and provide water for household use. Though they lived long ago, the Babylonians had a surprisingly "civilized" lifestyle. They lived in neatly laid-out cities and enjoyed bustling business and a thriving culture.

The people of the Babylonian Empire worshiped powerful gods and goddesses, but not one single supreme deity. Tiamat is the Babylonian creator of heaven and earth. She is the embodiment of primeval Chaos, from which the order of all life springs. Marduk, a later god, defeated Tiamat in battle. This story is a mythical retelling of a cultural shift within Babylon. When the newer patriarchy overtook the older matriarchal system, the people described the change figuratively as a male deity defeating a female deity. Other important Babylonian deities include the father-sky god Anu, the mother goddess Aruru (who created people), the water-god Ea and the goddess of the seasonal cycles, Inanna. Inanna is perhaps the best known of Babylon's deities. She was important to the Babylonians, but by no means is She the only deity they worshiped.

CANAANITES

The Canaanite Empire spanned a region that includes modern Israel, Lebanon, and Syria. This region is also called the Levant. The civilization we refer to as Canaan flourished from about 3000 to 1800 B.C.E. This same area re-emerged later as the center of the Phoenician Empire (see page 49). The people who live in the Levant have led similar lifestyles for thousands of years. Except for the intrusion of electricity and automobiles, people in this area have long led a simple life of farming and skilled crafts that has changed little since the earliest civilizations in the area.

The Canaanites worshiped the Goddess under the names Astarte, Ashtoreth, and Anath, and they called to the gods Baal (Master of the Heavenly House) and El. Astarte's shrine at Byblos dates back to Neolithic times, even before any cities were built in the area. Often the ancient Canaanites referred to their deities simply as Adath (the Lady) and Adon (the Lord). The Hebrews who lived in the same area borrowed the Canaanite term Adon and used it later in Greek form as Adonai, to refer to their god Yahweh. The Canaanites worshiped the goddess Hubal at a black meteorite in a temple in the city of Mecca. Cultural changes to patriarchy eventually forced the re-imaging of Hubal as a god, though Her/His practical worship changed little. In fact, that sacred meteorite still sits in Mecca today, in an Islamic mosque, but now it is honored as being sacred to the prophet Mohammed and the Moslem deity Allah.

CELTS

The Celts were a loose-knit group of tribes that stretched across Europe, united by a common culture and similar religious practices. Though sometimes referred to as the Celtic Empire, the Celts were never unified under a single ruler. Rather, they were distinct from other European peoples due to their unique culture and society.

The Celts populated the British Isles as well as a large portion of continental Europe, from parts of modern-day Spain in the west all the way to the Ukraine in the east. Celtic civilization also spread widely through the Celts' numerous trade routes, leaving outposts in Italy, Greece, and Asia Minor. The height of Celtic civilization was from about 500 B.C.E. to the turn of the millennium, when Caesar's Roman troops destroyed the Celtic tribal confederacies. Even under Roman rule, a distinct Celtic culture continued until about 300 C.E. The Celts were a pastoral people, amassing cattle as a form of wealth. They farmed the rich European soil and became quite skilled at the arts of music and metalworking.

Celtic deities included goddesses of sacred rivers and springs and gods of the forest, field, and wild animals. Familiar goddess names include Brigid or Brigantia, Boand, Grania, and Morrigu. Gods include the horned gods Cernunnos and Herne, as well as gods of the seasonal cycles such as Aengus, Dagda, Bran, and Lugh. We have more names for British Isles Celtic deities than for continental European ones simply because there are more extensive written records from the British Isles than from the continent. The continental Celts had a rich and varied religious life, but unfortunately we do not have very extensive records of the names by which they called their deities.

CRETANS

Crete is a small island off the southern coast of Greece. A mere 150 miles long by 50 miles wide at its widest point, Crete was home to the farthest-reaching mercantile civilization in the ancient world. The ancient Cretans traded with people as far away as the British Isles and Scandinavia to the west and India and China to the east. Though the island was first settled around 5000 B.C.E. or possibly earlier, Cretan society did not reach its zenith until 2500 B.C.E. Crete remained a great power for a thousand years until a combination of natural disasters and political upheavals allowed the mainland Greeks to take over the island and its culture around 1500 B.C.E.

The Cretans lived a lifestyle many in the modern world would envy. They enjoyed paved streets, indoor plumbing, and remarkably safe cities. Famed for their ability as traders and businesspeople, the Cretans also excelled at artwork, pottery, and gold-smithing. Sometimes the ancient Cretan people are referred to as Minoans. This term stems from the ideas of Sir Arthur Evans, the Victorian-era Englishman who excavated a large portion of the Cretan city of Knossos. He named the Cretan people after Minos, the Cretan priest-king who embodied the sacred Moon-Bull.

But the era of the Moon-Bull was only a small part of the history of ancient Crete, so scholars these days prefer to call these people Cretans, after the name of their island home.

As happened with many ancient civilizations, the names of the Cretan gods are lost in the dust of antiquity. Fortunately, the ancient Greeks took an interest in the Cretan mythos and recorded many names of Cretan deities in their own Greek writings. Though not exact matches for the original Cretan names, they do give us a close approximation of the deity names the Cretans used. The GreatMother goddess, Rhea, presided over a grand pantheon of Cretan deities. For many millennia She ruled alone, with no consort, as Great Mother Ocean. Eventually, She acquired a consort who took the various shapes of a serpent, stag, goat, or bull. Her consort, called the Minotauros, gave rise to the cult of the Moon-Bull, which grew until the Minotauros overshadowed the rest of Crete's deities and even infiltrated the pantheon of the mainland Greeks. Crete's extensive pantheon included the goddesses Ariadne (Fate), Eleithyia (the Midwife), and Ananke (Necessity) as well as the gods Cronos (Father Time) and Zagreus (the Sacrifice). The Cretans believed that all the goddesses were simply faces of the one Goddess, and all gods faces of the one God.

EGYPTIANS

Long before the time of the great pharaonic dynasties, the Egyptian Empire was originally two separate kingdoms. The Lower Kingdom occupied the area around the Nile delta on the northern sea coast, while the Upper Kingdom was farther south along the Nile (upriver, hence its name).

Ancient Spellcraft

The unification of the two areas in approximately 3000 B.C.E. marks the beginning of the dynasties of ancient Egypt. The power and grandeur of the great Egyptian Empire continued for millennia, finally fading with the conquest of Egypt by Alexander the Great in 332 B.C.E.

Similar to the Cretan pantheon, the rich and complex Egyptian pantheon is known largely through Greek translations of the deities' names. However, some reconstruction of the ancient Egyptian language has been accomplished, so I will offer Egyptian names where they are commonly used. Among the earliest Egyptian deities is the cobra goddess Ua Zit, represented as the uraeus (upright cobra head) on the pharaoh's crown. The cobra is the Egyptian hieroglyph for "goddess" because, after all, the cobra is Her oldest face in Egypt. The cobra symbol includes the meanings of mystic wisdom and insight, which are the gifts of the Goddess. The Egyptian hieroglyph for the Great Mother Creatress is three cauldrons; so even in Egypt we see the concept of the triple goddess who creates all that is. Egyptian goddesses included the powerful figures of Au Set (Greek Isis), Hwt-Hrw (Hathor), Maat, and Nut. Gods included Au Sar (Osiris), Horus, and Thoth. By approximately 1300 B.C.E. two Sun gods, Amun and Ra, had been united into the deity Amun-Ra, whose worship then became very prominent. While Egypt never actually became monotheistic, most other deities paled beside the all-powerful Amun-Ra.

ETRUSCANS

The Etruscan civilization spread over west central Italy around the Tiber River in an area then called Etruria.

Etruscan civilization was the most advanced culture in Italy before the Roman Empire. In fact, the Etruscans were the direct predecessors of the Roman Empire. The Etruscans had developed a distinct culture by about 900 B.C.E. but declined rapidly by about 400 B.C.E. as the Romans took power. Like the Celts, the Etruscans had no centralized government. They were a loose confederation of city-states held together by religious and political ties. Due to their lack of centralization, they were easily overwhelmed by the highly organized Romans. Etruscan civilization included highly skilled metalsmiths who created beautiful jewelry, household metalworks, and sculptures. Though the Romans far exceeded the Etruscans in many regards, most historians consider that the Romans never equaled the Etruscans in this particular skill.

The Etruscans left few written records and their language is still not very well understood. Fortunately, the Romans, who traded extensively with the Etruscans and eventually took over their territory, recorded much about the Etruscans' deities. Unfortunately, however, the Romans equated most of the Etruscan deities with their own gods and goddesses, recording only Roman names for them. So, for instance, we know the Etruscans worshiped deities who were the equivalent of the Roman Jupiter, Juno, Mars, Apollo, and Venus. We also know of the Etruscan-named love goddess Turan and the sky god Tin from inscriptions in the Etruscans' native language. Etruscan temples had an underground section that devotees could enter as if they were entering the Goddess' womb. These man-made caves (called *mundus*, meaning earth or womb) were replacements for the natural caves used as shrines before temples were built in the towns.

Ancient Spellcraft

GREEKS

The ancient Greek Empire included all of the modern country of Greece as well as parts of Asia Minor and the Aegean islands. Classical, or Hellenic, Greek civilization flourished from about 1000 B.C.E., through the time of Alexander the Great in the 300s B.C.E., until the decline and eventual takeover by Rome in about 150 B.C.E. Throughout the heyday of Hellenic civilization, Greece remained a collection of independent city-states that each ruled a limited region. Power shifted from region to region over time and never consolidated into a central Greek government the way it did in the Roman Empire. In fact, the regional rulers within the Greek civilization often fought with each other, but they all considered themselves undeniably Greek. The ancient Greeks were bound together not by their government, but by ties of culture and religion.

Thanks to the many writings passed down to us from classical Greek authors, Greek deities are still familiar to us today. From Zeus and Hera on Mt. Olympus, to Athena and Apollo on the Acropolis, and Aphrodite and Poseidon in the sea, Greek goddesses and gods trace their way through myth and ritual all the way into our modern culture. Their names and their stories have become an integral part of contemporary western culture so that they live on in a very real way in the modern world.

HITTITES

The Hittites lived in Asia Minor, in the region of modern-day Turkey and Syria, from about 1700 to 1200 B.C.E.

They were a patriarchal, ambitious people who rapidly took over a large portion of Asia Minor and regularly attempted to invade the Babylonians. A loose confederacy under the rule of various warrior-kings, the Hittite Empire broke up due to invasion from neighboring nations. The Hittites stood out in comparison to their neighbors in the Middle East because of the rigid patriarchal structure of their society. Other Middle Eastern cultures of the time allowed women a great deal of autonomy and power. In terms of daily life, the Hittites lived very much like the other people around them; raising crops, herding sheep and goats in the open desert spaces, and conducting business in the cities. The main thing the Hittites are remembered for, though, is their warlike attitude toward the surrounding civilizations.

The Hittites assimilated a number of Babylonian and other regional deities into their pantheon. We cannot be certain which deities belonged originally to the Hittites and which were borrowed from other cultures they contacted. We do know, however, that every culture that touched the Hittites donated their deities, in one form or another, to the Hittite pantheon. The "thousand deities of Hatti" (as described in a Hittite inscription) were headed by Kumarbi, Father of all the gods, and Hannahanna, Mother of all the gods. One of the most well known Hittite goddesses is Wurusemu, the Sun goddess of the city of Arinna. The Hittites also called to the Babylonian gods Ellil and Ea, and goddesses Ninlil, Ereshkigal, and Ishtar.

PHOENICIANS

The Phoenician Empire was the later outgrowth of the Canaanite settlements (see page 42) in the Middle East. Also located in the Levant, the Phoenicians flourished from 1800 to 600 B.C.E., at which point they were absorbed into the conquering Persian Empire. They were a seagoing mercantile people whose trading contacts spanned the whole Mediterranean, westward to Spain, and probably even around to the British Isles. The Phoenicians never called themselves by this name, though. The term Phoenician is the name the Greeks gave to these people with whom they frequently traded. The term comes from the Greek word for the famous reddish-purple dye that the Phoenicians used on the fabric they sold. The dye was fabulously expensive because it had to be made by hand in very small quantities from a mollusk found on the beaches of the Phoenician coastline. It was this expensive dye, "Phoenician purple," that made the color purple famous as an attribute of royalty. For the most part, this was because the dye was so expensive that only royalty could afford it. But the dye also had a sacred meaning.

Though we now refer to it as purple, the original color was actually closer to bloodred, the color of life-giving blood and especially of the Goddess's sacred menstrual blood. The wearing of this color in the ancient world was often restricted to members of the priesthood, or royalty, who represented the gods on Earth. In the later Roman Empire, there were laws that restricted the amount of purple a person could wear on their garments depending on their station in life. So, something as simple as a fabric dye gave the Phoenicians a legacy that lives on today. In terms of the specific deities they worshiped, the Phoenicians carried on the traditions of their Canaanite ancestors. Their elaborate temples and religious services centered around just a

The Ancient World

few deities, including the goddesses Astarte and Baalat, and the gods Adonis and Baal.

ROMANS

The Roman Empire began as a collection of settlements along the Tiber River in modern-day Italy. By 500 B.C.E., these cities had developed a consolidated central government. Eventually the Roman Empire grew to encompass the entire Mediterranean basin, the better part of Europe, and western Asia Minor. The Roman Empire flourished under the central leadership of a long string of emperors, a ruling Senate, and a complex system of local governors. In the third century C.E., the empire split into eastern and western divisions and the legacy of ancient Rome crumbled.

Many of the familiar Roman deities are simply Romanized versions of Greek goddesses and gods. The Romans copied many aspects of Greek culture, especially Greek religion and art. Within the Roman pantheon you will meet Jupiter and Juno, Mars and Venus, Diana and Apollo, and a host of others. Much of modern Europe owes a great deal of cultural influence to the Roman Empire. Even today the Roman myths are retold in schools and Roman deity names pop up in literature, advertising, and even daily conversation.

SUMERIANS

The highly developed ancient Sumerian civilization spread across the flat desert land that is now in the southern part of Iraq. This region between the Tigris and Euphrates

Ancient Spellcraft

Rivers in modern Iraq is referred to as Mesopotamia, or the Fertile Crescent. The Babylonian Empire (see page 41) occupied northern Mesopotamia. The Sumerian civilization filled the southern portion all the way down to the Persian Gulf. The Sumerians flourished from about 3000 to 1800 B.C.E., although their settlements began at least as early as 5000 B.C.E. In fact, Sumer may have been the first civilization to arise on Earth. As with many of the ancient cultures in the West, Sumer was a collection of city-states, each with its own ruler and often, its own deities.

It is the Sumerians who gave us the famous epic of the mythological hero Gilgamesh. Along with Gilgamesh, in the Sumerian pantheon we meet the goddesses Ninhursag, Inanna, and Ereshkigal, as well as the gods Enlil, Enki, Dumuzi, and Nergal. The complex Sumerian pantheon combines the familiar and powerful main deities with individual faces of the Goddess and God who protected each Sumerian city and ruled over its crafts and businesses.

Though these ancient civilizations spanned a large geographic region and a great length of time, they had much in common with each other and with us in our modern world. They all raised families, worked at jobs, and hoped for a bright future. Just as we do, they wished for prosperity, romance, fertility, protection, and healing. They sought a glimpse into the future through divination to better plan their lives. And for all this, they called on their deities—goddesses and gods whose power sustained the spirituality of these ancient cultures and whose power still lives on today. Call the names of these ancient deities, asking for their aid in your spellwork, and you will touch the far-distant past and bring it magickally into your life.

CHAPTER 3

 # Prosperity

prosperity: n. "the condition of being successful or thriving, esp. economic well-being" (Webster's New Collegiate Dictionary, 918)

Prosperity is a powerful word that symbolizes many different things to different people. The word *prosperity* comes from an Indo-European root *(prospere)* that means "according to one's hope" (Watkins, 63). In other words, prosperity is the sum of the things you hope or wish for. For some people, prosperity is a successful business, a high-paying job, or a more meaningful or fulfilling job. For others, it is a secure home, or the piece of rural land they've always wanted, or a new car, or an overflowing pantry. Prosperity encompasses many things that make people feel secure and well-off.

People tend to equate prosperity with money, but what they really want are the things that money can buy. So instead of visualizing money, try thinking about what prosperity really is *for you*. If you had all that money, what would you buy? Money is just an intermediate step, a means to an end, and the end is prosperity. So focus on the end result, the thing that really means prosperity to you—not the money. The universe takes the shortest, most efficient route to give you what you ask for. For example, if, to you, prosperity means driving a newer car, the universe may find it easier to have someone give you their old car when they buy a new one, rather than giving you the money to buy a car. So don't tell the universe what path to take. It knows better than you do. Just tell it where you want to go and it will take you there.

Regardless of your vision of prosperity, this section will provide you with a wide-ranging collection of simple spells and charms to bring prosperity to your own doorstep. Use them to fill your life with the many varieties of abundance the world has to offer.

A LIFE OF ABUNDANCE

In addition to money, prosperity includes abundance in all aspects of life. For the ancients, the most visible sign of prosperity was food—healthy livestock, burgeoning gardens, and overflowing pantries. Because food is such a primal need, these images still have power today. In this sense, prosperity may mean plenty of food, enough income to pay all the bills, or a spacious and secure home. Prosperity can enter our lives through many different avenues. The following spells offer a variety of visions of prosperity to aid you in fulfilling your dreams.

A Prosperous Harvest

The goddess Rhea has cared for Her children in civilizations all around the eastern end of the Mediterranean for millennia. She is the primal Great Mother who is also the death-bringing Crone, the goddess of the great cycle of birth,

Prosperity

life, death, and rebirth. Her consort, Cronos, is the god of the fields, the personification of the abundance of the harvest. He is the life-sustaining grain that must itself die in order to provide food for us and thus complete one round of the Great Mother's cycle.

The Cretans called the goddess Rhea also by the name Cronia, or Mother Time. She originally wielded the castrating moon-sickle, or scythe, its blade shaped like the crescent moon that represented Her ever-changing cycles. This is the instrument with which her consort, the Heavenly Father, was 'reaped.' Rhea, then, was the Grim Reaper, with Cronos (Father Time) as her consort. Far from the bleak and distasteful image of the modern Grim Reaper, Rhea lovingly fulfilled a necessary task in the natural cycle of things. And Her actions brought prosperity into the lives of her people—a bountiful harvest, full larders, and joyful lives.

Rhea does require a sacrifice as payment for prosperity. In ancient times, the sacrifice was the god of the fields, or perhaps his earthly counterpart, a priest or king. In modern times, such a sacrifice is neither acceptable nor necessary. Rhea simply requires that we give fully of ourselves and are willing

Ancient Spellcraft

to do the work necessary to earn the bounty that She dispenses. It is hard, sweaty work to reap grain from a field. Think, then, how you will work to gain prosperity, and what you are willing to give up (procrastination? disorganization? denial?) in order to attain it. Take care, though, to take this seriously. Once you have written down your promises and given them to the Goddess, She will pay special attention to see that you keep your word.

The Spell

What you will need:

- ✦ Parchment and a pen for writing down your sacrifice.
- ✦ A cup of red wine.
- ✦ A fireplace, campfire pit, cauldron, or similar fire container (a hibachi or barbecue grill will do in a pinch) with a small fire burning in it. Please don't use a candle—the parchment could blaze up and catch nearby items, including your clothing and hair, on fire. Use a fire that is burning in a container or fireplace large enough to safely hold the burning parchment.

Performing the spell:

Set the wine to one side of the fire. Place the parchment and pen in front of you, quiet your mind, and concentrate on your purpose. Envision all the different kinds of prosperity you wish to bring into your life. Call to the Goddess:

"I call to you, Rhea Cronia, Mother Time. Your wisdom and generosity sustain life and fill my heart with joy. I thank You for the gifts You have already given

Prosperity

me, and I beg Your patience and generosity that I might ask Your favor tonight."

Think very carefully about what you will sacrifice, what you will give in order to receive abundance and prosperity in your life. When you have it clear in your mind, write your sacrifice down on the parchment. Read it over to be sure this is something you are truly willing to do. Once you have burned the parchment, you have made a contract with the Goddess and you may not go back on your word. When you are sure, pick up the cup of wine and hold it over the fire.

"The Earth, body of the Goddess, has poured out Her life that I might flourish."

Pour some wine onto the fire, leaving some still in the cup. Watch the wine flame and hear it sizzle in the fire. Now take the parchment in your hand and hold it over the fire.

"Holy Rhea, Mother of us all, I offer You a sacrifice, that I may taste Your abundance and know Your plenty. I give back to You something I hold dear. Accept this, my token of gratitude, as I return to the Earth a portion of what I take from it."

Read aloud what you have written on the parchment. With due thought, drop the parchment in the fire. Watch it blaze up, burn, and turn to ash. Contemplate the promise you have just made in return for prosperity in your life. Pick up the cup of wine. Drink the remains to seal your spell.

"The wine I drink is the life-blood of the grape. I drink it in thanksgiving for the bounty I receive from the Great Mother. What you give me, Holy Rhea, I receive in gratitude and love. I give thanks for Your bounty, and I remember what I have given up that I may have what I desire."

Put out the fire in silence.

Lady of the Corn-Ripe Yellow Hair

The Greek goddess Demeter rules over the fields and the storehouses, meting out scarcity to those who have disappointed Her and prosperity to those She likes. Her attributes are grain (often referred to as corn, but barley is more historically accurate) and poppies. As the goddess of the agricultural cycle, She embodies harvest and death as well as birth and life. Poppies represent death in a way we do not often think of it in the modern world. Poppy seeds bring a sleep much like death, but they are also beautiful. Demeter's followers revered every stage of the cycle of the universe as beautiful.

As the grain goddess, Demeter watched over the whole process of growing, harvesting, storing, and using the grain. Once grain was taken from the field, the kernels had to be separated from the rest of the dried plant. Nowadays this is accomplished with fancy machinery, but in the ancient world, elbow grease and simple tools sufficed. The first part of the separation process is called threshing. The dried grain is placed on the floor of the threshing room and beaten with wooden flails to loosen the kernels from their outer covering. Then the broken bits are placed in shallow baskets and fanned so the lightweight chaff blows away and the heavier kernels of grain are left. This fanning process is called winnowing. We still use this term today when we refer to "winnowing out" people or items from a group.

Demeter's festival was both a solemn and a joyous occasion in ancient Greece. It lasted a full nine days, during which time regular work ceased so the people could focus on the abundance with which they had been blessed. You, too, can reap the harvest of Demeter's abundance with this simple spell and respect for Her great power.

The Spell

What you will need:

- ✦ A loaf of bread that you have baked yourself. If you're unfamiliar with baking bread, the simplest method is to use frozen bread dough from your grocery store. Just bake it according to the package directions.
- ✦ Symbols of Demeter—grain, flour, and poppies. These can be pictures or the real items.
- ✦ Symbols of prosperity. You can cut pictures out of magazines or use actual items (money, jewelry, food, whatever evokes prosperity to you).

Performing the spell:

Arrange an area in which to perform this spell, preferably outside. The ancient Greeks performed similar rites in the grain fields and grain storage rooms, surrounded by the

Ancient Spellcraft

barley that is Demeter's abundance. Set up the symbols of Demeter all in one place as an altar. Arrange the symbols of prosperity so that you are surrounded by them as you stand in front of Demeter's altar. It is best to set up your altar area while the bread is baking, so the bread will still be warm when you perform the spell.

Hold the loaf of bread in your hands and stand surrounded by the prosperity symbols you have chosen. Quiet your mind and concentrate on the prosperity that surrounds you, just as the ancient Greeks stood surrounded by Demeter's harvest bounty. Think of all this prosperity in the present, here and now, not at some distant time in the future. Now break the loaf of bread in half. Place half of it on Demeter's altar, for that is Her share. Hold the other half in your hands as you complete the spell, saying:

> "May I stand beside Demeter's altar. May She let me dig my winnowing fan into Her huge piles of grain. May She stand smiling by me with sheaves of grain and poppies. May Her abundance be mine also."

Eat a piece of the warm bread and taste the prosperity in your life. Meditate for a while, focusing on your vision of prosperity. The symbols that surround you will help you to concentrate. When you are done, clean up your tools. Eat the remainder of your half of the bread, but do not eat the bread you have given to Demeter. Leave it out overnight so that She may enjoy it. Then you may add it to your compost, bury it, or feed it to the ducks at your local park. Just be sure to return it to the earth, which is where it came from in the first place.

A Full Cornucopia

Fortuna, the Roman goddess of good fortune, is often pictured with an overflowing cornucopia in her arms or at her feet. Originally a Greek symbol, the cornucopia is a large horn-shaped container that magickally fills itself with whatever its owner requests. It is thought originally to have been the horn of the lunar cow- or goat-goddess, whose curved horn symbolizes the changing phases of the Moon. As symbols of abundance and prosperity, cornucopias are frequently seen in modern America around Thanksgiving time. Fortuna's cornucopia fulfills much the same role as the Goddess's vase or cauldron in other ancient traditions. It represents Her overflowing, never-ending abundance. We are all heir to this abundance. All we need do is ask and She will share it with us.

The Spell

What you will need:

- ✦ A cornucopia. This needs to be a real one, not a picture. Craft and gift shops often carry cornucopia-shaped baskets.

- Nine small items that represent prosperity to you. They should all fit into the cornucopia together, filling it to overflowing.

Performing the spell:

This is a simple spell but it takes nine days to perform. The number nine is sacred to Fortuna, so repeating the spell nine days in a row makes it especially powerful and fortuitous. This is a form of the ancient Roman *votum*, or nine-day spell. At the end of the nine days, when you have completed the spell, set the filled cornucopia where it can remain undisturbed as a reminder of the prosperity that Fortuna brings to you.

To begin, place the cornucopia where it can remain for the full nine days of the spell's working. Line up the nine prosperity items in front of it. On each of nine consecutive days, do the following:

Pick up one of the prosperity items and hold it up, saying, "Sweet Fortuna, may you shine your good fortune on me. May you fill my cornucopia to overflowing and pour out the blessings of prosperity on me every day of my life." Place the prosperity item in the cornucopia. Envision the kind of prosperity that particular object symbolizes. Picture the prosperity overflowing into your life.

Repeat the spell each night until you have put all the prosperity items in the cornucopia and it is full. Then put the full cornucopia where it will remain undisturbed as a reminder of your spell and of Fortuna's generosity.

My Cup Runneth Over

The milk-giving cow, with horns that symbolized the phases of the Moon, embodied prosperity and abundance

Prosperity

to the ancient Cretans. As the lunar goddess Europa poured out her life-giving milk to create the Milky Way in the starry sky, so Her earthly counterpart pours out abundance to human beings. The Cretans poured libations of cow's milk and red wine to symbolize the milk and blood that support life. Pouring out a liquid is sympathetic magick, representing the Goddess's pouring out of abundance to us from Her bounty. Offer the libation in this spell, then, to bring an outpouring of Europa's abundance into your life.

The Spell

What you will need:

- ✦ A pitcher.
- ✦ Cow's milk (whole milk, please—you want the cream of prosperity, don't you?). Fill the pitcher to the brim with the milk, as full as you can get it without spilling. This represents the fullness of the Goddess's abundance.
- ✦ A bowl big enough to hold all the milk in the pitcher, if you're going to do this spell indoors.

Performing the spell:

Perform this spell when the full Moon rides high in the sky, clearly visible above you. This spell is best done outdoors in the light of the Moon, pouring the libation onto the ground and hence giving it back to the Goddess as Mother Earth. If weather prevents you from working outside, pour the libation into the bowl and save it until you can go outside and return it to the Earth. If you are performing this spell for your family rather than just yourself, be sure to change the pronouns to plural in the words of the spell.

Ancient Spellcraft

Hold the pitcher up and let the moonlight fall on it, reflecting on the surface of the milk. Call to the Goddess:

"Europa, gracious Goddess of the full face of the Moon, by Your horns I know the passing of the days and the turning of the cycles. Pour out Your abundance on me, I pray, that I may know the fullness of Your bounty as I know the fullness of the Moon."

Pour the milk slowly out onto the ground, chanting the following as you do so:

"From the Goddess flows life-giving milk in Her bounty. May abundance flow to me till my pitcher is full."

When the pitcher is empty, turn it upside down on the ground to show the Goddess that you have emptied it. Thank Her for Her gifts to you:

"I thank you, Europa, gracious goddess of the full face of the Moon. I thank You for the knowledge of the passing of the days and the turning of the cycles. I thank You for Your gifts of abundance in my life."

Leave the pitcher where it sits until the Moon has set below the horizon.

Getting rid of bad luck to make way for prosperity

Sometimes a string of negative circumstances can make you feel like you're never going to achieve prosperity. Even if the bad luck is just that—random chaos rearing its ugly head in your life through no fault of yours—it can still turn you into a pessimist. Your mindset is a large part of what is

Prosperity

necessary to achieve prosperity in the first place. The spells that follow have the aim of getting rid of bad luck, misfortune, and other negativity in order to make room in your life for prosperity. Use these spells to return your mindset to hope and optimism so you're ready to enjoy the prosperity the gods send your way.

A Clean Sweep

For millennia, the ancient Greeks turned to the grain goddess Demeter for harvest-time prosperity. But before they could store the abundant harvested grain, Demeter's followers had to clean out the storehouses to make room for the new harvest. Any old grain left in the storehouses could spoil the new crop when it was brought in. They cleaned the storehouses reverently as part of the sacred process of preparing for the harvest. Demeter's followers devoted themselves to sweeping out the grain storage rooms dedicated to Her, to make them absolutely spotless and empty before the new grain was brought into them. Removing all the remains of the old grain and literally making a clean sweep makes room for new prosperity and abundance. This is an excellent spell to work when you have had bad luck or a string of unfortunate circumstances, and you wish to begin again and enter prosperity.

The Spell
What you will need:
- A broom and dustpan.
- A container for the sweepings. This should be something the dust and trash are not likely to spill out of, such as a small box.
- A shovel or trowel.

Ancient Spellcraft

- ✦ A place to dig a hole in the ground, to bury the sweepings. If you will be using someone else's land, be sure to get their permission first.

Performing the spell:

Perform this spell at your place of business if you seek prosperity specifically in business, or at your home if you seek prosperity throughout your whole life. Begin by quieting your mind and focusing on the concept of removing old debris in order to make way for prosperity. Ask Demeter for Her assistance:

"Demeter of the corn-ripe yellow hair, I humbly ask Your aid as I clear away the dust of past misfortune to make way for new prosperity."

Now carefully sweep your entire house or place of business and collect the sweepings in the dustpan. Transfer the sweepings to the box and take a long look at what you are removing from your life. As you examine the dust, dirt, and trash, imagine that it contains all the misfortune and lack of prosperity from your life. Now take the box outside. Dig a hole with the shovel or trowel, pour the sweepings into the hole, and cover them over with dirt. Go back into the place you swept out and complete the spell:

"Bountiful Demeter, I have cleared away the old rubbish. This place is now clean and empty, ready to receive Your bounty and prosperity. I thank you for your aid, bountiful Demeter."

Fly Away

The ancient Cretans considered birds to be messengers of the gods. Birds in general, but especially doves, hawks,

Prosperity

and crows, were thought to carry human requests to the heavens where the gods resided. Birds also brought messages and blessings down from the gods to Earth. Due to their role as carriers of messages to and from the gods, birds were also thought to have the ability to carry bad luck and poverty away from a person so that he or she could enjoy prosperity and abundance in life. This simple spell calls on birds in this capacity, to help you remove negativity from your life and make room for prosperity.

The Spell

What you will need:

- ✦ Breadcrumbs or birdseed.
- ✦ An outdoor area where birds can congregate.

Performing the spell:

Put a handful or two of breadcrumbs or birdseed into a container. Quiet your mind and think about the bad luck and negativity in your life that is blocking the way for prosperity. Hold the container in your hands and visualize all that negativity draining into the crumbs or birdseed. Take as long as you need for this visualization. Make sure you release all the negativity from your life so it flows freely into the breadcrumbs or birdseed.

Now take the container out to the place you have chosen to feed the birds. Spread the crumbs or seed out for the birds and call to them:

"Birds of the air, messengers of the gods, come take this negativity from me. Carry it back to the gods whence it came, so that there will be room in my life for prosperity."

You may wait and watch as the birds come and carry away all the crumbs or seed. Rest assured, this spell will not harm the birds. The negativity is not theirs. They are only messengers, carrying it away from you so prosperity can fill your life.

Brush It Off

The ancient Celts believed that the birch tree had a special ability to drive away bad luck, including the kinds of circumstances that keep prosperity out of our lives. Birch is the tree of the first month of the year in the Druidic calendar. Beginning right after Winter Solstice, Birch month is the time when the days begin to grow longer again after the darkness of Winter. At this time of year, the Celts used birch twigs to sweep away negativity (misfortune, evil spirits, gloom, lingering illness) from their homes and lives in preparation for the bounty of Spring. The simple homemade broom they used eventually evolved into the form of the besom, or magickal broom. A Celtic besom is made with birch twigs bound to an ash handle with strips of willow.

Prosperity

The ancient Celts also believed that loud noises would drive bad luck away. They rang bells and banged on pots in order to frighten evil spirits and misfortune away. This tradition has survived, albeit in a slightly warped form, in the Christian belief that ringing bells loudly will drive witches away. So pick up your broom and bells, and drive away bad luck to make way for the good!

The Spell

What you will need:

- Birch twigs, preferably ones that have fallen from the tree. If you must cut twigs from a living tree, be sure to ask its permission first. A tree is a living thing, deserving of respect. Either tie the birch twigs together in a bundle that roughly resembles a broom, or tie them onto the "business end" of a broom.
- Noisemakers. Bells and gongs are good, but you could also use the time-honored combination of a large spoon banging on pots and pans.

Performing the spell:

Since this spell calls for sweeping and making loud noises at the same time, it will be easiest to have someone (or several someones) help you. Choose the area you will be cleansing—your office, place of business, home—wherever you want to clear away negativity in order to make room for prosperity. Mentally define a path around the edge of the

Ancient Spellcraft

area you intend to cleanse. This is where you will walk as you perform the spell.

Collect all your tools where you intend to begin the path. Quiet your mind. Focus your thoughts on the negativity that you are banishing. If several people will be performing this spell together, you may wish to describe out loud the things you will be banishing. This way, the other participants will be better able to visualize the impact of the spell. Now, using the birch twigs as a broom, sweep vigorously around the edge of the area you are cleansing. As you sweep, visualize the negativity being flung far away by the birch twigs.

At the same time, someone else follows the same path, making loud noises with the bells, rattles, or other noisemakers. They may shout at the same time. While making all this racket, they visualize the negativity running rapidly away, fleeing from the loud noise. Go around the whole perimeter of the area at least one full circuit with the birch twigs and noisemakers. You may go around as many times as you feel are necessary in order to fully banish the negativity. When you are done, wait until all is quiet again. Now visualize (or share out loud with your helpers) the empty space filling up with prosperity in its many glorious forms.

SUCCESS IN THE BUSINESS WORLD

People have traded and run businesses for millennia. For as long as there have been businesses, people have asked their favorite deities for success in the business world. Prosperity in business encompasses financial success and much more—contented employees and customers, a good reputation, and

Prosperity

a thriving business that has the resources to give back to the community that supports it. Use the spells in this section to bring prosperity into your business, whether you work for someone else or run your own company.

Teach a Man to Fish

The Sumerian god Enki is credited with teaching people how to build irrigation canals and thus, how to grow enough crops to have surplus to trade . . . and make a profit . . . and prosper. With the building of the first canals, Enki was said to make the Tigris and Euphrates Rivers "eat together." Enki is both a Fire and a Water god, born of the primal Cosmic Waters, seen as a Sun rising from the waters (sunrise over the Persian Gulf, perhaps?). Being from a water source, Enki accepts fish as offerings. And since He is also identified with Fire, the fish offered to Him are transported to His abode through Fire. Though often referred to as a burnt offering, this type of spell is more accurately called a Fire offering since it is given to a Fire god.

The Sumerians were among the earliest merchants and businesspeople in the ancient world, trading far and wide from Spain in the West to India in the East. They created

Ancient Spellcraft

canals and built a thriving, prosperous civilization in an arid, desert-like land. So if you're seeking an oasis, a source of energy and inspiration for the prosperity of your business, turn to Enki.

The Spell

What you will need:

- A fish. No kidding. A whole one, please, not fillets or steaks. It should still look like a fish. Most large supermarkets have a seafood section that sells whole fish such as trout. Go for something of a reasonable size. A 200-pound tuna isn't going to net you any more prosperity than a 1-pound trout.
- A barbecue grill, hibachi, or campfire. In other words, a place where you can cook (burn, actually) the fish. Please don't try this indoors, in a fireplace for example—you'll just fill your house with smoke and may start a dangerous fire. Outdoors, please, using something designed to hold fire and cook food.

Performing the spell:

Prepare the grill or fire on which you will offer the fish. Make sure it is hot enough to char the fish before you begin the spell. When the fire is ready, set the fish out in front of it and call to Enki:

> "I call to Enki, Lord of the Waters, Son of the Primal Sea. O You who brought the waters of prosperity into the hungry desert, I offer You this fish, food of the waters and food for a god."

Set the fish on the fire and watch as it heats up, then blackens and begins to smoke. As you watch, concentrate on your personal vision of prosperity for your business. When a steady column of smoke rises from the fish, call to Enki again:

"O Enki, Lord of the Waters, I send to You the smoke from this offering and I ask a favor of You. As You blessed the dry desert with flowing Water so the cities would prosper, please bless my business with prosperity overflowing."

Allow the fish to cook until it is totally charred and black. Douse your fire (or let the charcoal burn out, or turn off the gas grill) and allow the fish to cool completely before handling it. Preferably, dispose of the fish in the compost or bury it in your garden as fertilizer. Alternately, simply bury it in the dirt in a location that will remain undisturbed until the fish has decomposed and returned to the earth. Please don't throw the fish in the trash—that's disrespectful.

Working on Island Time

The ancient Cretans did remarkably well in business. They concentrated their enormous wealth back into their many businesses rather than spending it on an expensive military. They lived on a small island and let the rest of the world know that they weren't interested in military conquest. Instead, they conquered the known world through trade. The Cretans had the richest and farthest reaching mercantile empire of the ancient world. Prosperity was practically their middle name.

Over this vast trade empire ruled the great goddess Ariadne, and sacred to her was the saffron crocus. This lovely flower blooms so early in the Spring that it often pokes its beautifully colored head up through the snow. The crocus, then, is a reminder that Spring will come, no matter how cold Winter has been. The Cretan merchants eagerly awaited Spring each year. Their ships were grounded during the Winter and could not safely take to sea again until the vicious south wind abated in the Spring. In terms of business, the crocus symbolizes prosperity after hard times and hard work. The stigma (pollen-bearing parts) of the crocus gives us saffron, one of the costliest spices of both the ancient and modern world. The ancient Cretans offered saffron to Ariadne when asking her for prosperity. What better sacrifice to make to the Goddess who brings the Spring?

The Spell

What you will need:

- ✦ Saffron for the offering. It can often be found in the herb and spice section of large supermarkets, as well as in international markets and Indian (East Indian, not Native American) groceries.

Prosperity

- ✦ High quality red wine.
- ✦ Your best goblet or wine glass.
- ✦ A bowl for the libation, if you will be performing the spell indoors.

Performing the spell:

The Cretans would have performed this spell at an altar or shrine, either in a temple or in their home. At indoor shrines, they poured their libations into large bowls, and at outdoor shrines, they poured their libations onto the ground. You can set up a Cretan-style altar on a table in your house or on any flat surface outdoors. The Cretans did not display figurines of the Goddess on their altars since they considered their priestess to be the living embodiment of the Goddess.

You can leave your altar bare except for the items needed for this spell, or you can add flowers (especially crocuses and lilies), incense, and/or a labrys in some form (jewelry or artwork, for example). Set all your tools and ingredients on the altar before you begin. Quiet your mind and concentrate on your purpose. Call to Ariadne, holding up first the wine and then the saffron as you name them:

"Holy Ariadne, Spinner of the golden thread of fate, Weaver of the web of life, I call to You. I have brought You sweet wine and precious saffron, both dear to You. Please accept my gift and bring Your prosperity to my business."

Fill up the goblet with wine and sprinkle the saffron on top of the wine. Watch the golden threads of saffron swirl in the wine and envision the prosperity you desire for your business. When you have the vision clear in your mind, hold up the cup and silently give thanks to Ariadne for the many blessings you have already received. Pour out the saffron wine as a libation to Her. If you are outside, pour it onto the ground. If you are indoors, pour it into the bowl. Hold the cup upside down until the last drop falls and the cup is completely empty. Then set the goblet upside down on the altar, saying:

> "Holy Ariadne, I have emptied this cup to You, a thankful libation of fine wine and precious saffron. As I have given generously to You, so may You give generously to me."

Meditate for a few moments on the vision of your prosperous business. When you are through, clean up your altar and put away your tools. If you poured the libation into a bowl rather than onto the earth, leave the bowl out overnight before respectfully disposing of the contents. Be sure to put it in a place where it will remain undisturbed.

Advice From the Experts

The Phoenicians are the originators of worldwide trade monopolies and put a great deal of energy into spirituality for business purposes. Sacred to their culture was the mythical creature called the hippocampus. The hippocampus had the head, body, and forelegs of a horse but the tail of a dolphin. This creature eventually came to represent the seagoing Phoenician merchants and traders on their coins and ships' banners. Great numbers of impressions of the hippocampus have been found on seals of documents and containers of trade goods.

To the Phoenicians, the hippocampus symbolized the riches of trade (the horse) plus the opportunity that sea voyages offered (the dolphin). This mystical creature was,

Prosperity

in effect, the good luck charm for Phoenician business. Make your own good luck charm and seal the hippocampus's promise of prosperity to your business.

The Spell

What you will need:

- A picture of a hippocampus.
- Modeling clay, preferably the kind that hardens in the air without baking.
- A pencil.
- A potato.
- A small paring knife or craft knife.
- Printed matter that represents your business (business card, brochure, flyer, etc.).
- Piece of parchment large enough to fold around your business materials.

Performing the spell:

In this spell you will make your own hippocampus seal, bless it, and use it to place the hippocampus's prosperous energy into your business. First, cut the potato in half. Then, using the picture as a guide, draw an outline of the hippocampus on the cut surface of the potato. Using the knife,

Ancient Spellcraft

carve away the potato from around the outline so that the shape of the hippocampus stands out from the end of the potato. This does not have to be a work of art, but it does need to be detailed enough for you to recognize the shape of the hippocampus in it. If this seems like a lot of work, it is. But the effort you put into this spell will be amply rewarded.

Now take your business materials and lay them on the parchment. Fold the parchment around them like an envelope so that they won't fall out. Take a golf-ball size piece of the modeling clay and roll it into a smooth ball. Set it on the parchment where the edges of the paper overlap. Press it down to seal the edges of the parchment together. Smooth the top of the clay and make sure it is bigger than the hippocampus you carved on the potato. Now bless the hippocampus seal and call on this mythical creature's powers to bring prosperity to your business. Hold the carving in your dominant hand as you say:

> "I call to the gracious gods, the 70 children of Asherah, and to Kothar-and-Khasis, the god of crafts, whose name means skillful-and-clever. I pray you, bless this seal which I have made. Let the power of the hippocampus work through it to bring prosperity to my business."

Now say the name of your business out loud and press the seal down into the clay so that it leaves a recognizable impression. Before you lift the seal up off the clay, say:

> "With the power of the hippocampus, I seal prosperity into my business."

Once again say the name of your business out loud. Now set the sealed parchment in a safe place and do not open it. You may save the carved potato to use again, or cook it and

Prosperity

eat the prosperity it promises. If you wish to dispose of it, do so at your own home (in the compost or buried in the ground). Don't let it leave your house in the garbage, since the hippocampus might take the prosperity with it.

As you can see, there are many different kinds of prosperity and many different ways to attain it. Prosperity can mean financial success or the simple physical abundance of food, shelter, and clothing. Removing negative influences and old habits can make room for prosperity to enter your life. People throughout the ancient world looked to their favorite deities for help in achieving their dreams of prosperity. You, too, can call on these powerful forces to bring abundance and prosperity into your life.

CHAPTER 5

 # ROMANCE

romance n. "an emotional attraction or aura; love affair"
(Webster's New Collegiate Dictionary, 996)

When we talk about romance these days, we're referring to relationships with those we love. But the word *romance* originally had nothing to do with love. It simply referred to the language that the ordinary people in France spoke during the Middle Ages, as opposed to the Latin that the church and legal authorities used in their business dealings. The term *romance* developed a meaning revolving around love due to the love ballads that the traveling singer-storytellers, the troubadours and trouvères, sang in the medieval French language (Romance, that is). The ballads they sang were all about noble, splendid, marvelous, courtly love. The term *roman* referred to the stories that made up these ballads. These were tales of chivalry and adventure, but especially love. So the term *romance* came to mean the courtship and emotions surrounding someone we care for deeply.

Love is always noble, splendid, and marvelous when we envision it, isn't it? That first spark of interest, the growing passion and chemistry between two people have fueled literature, politics, even wars, for millennia. Other things in

Ancient Spellcraft

life matter little without someone to share them with. For those who do not have a romantic partner, finding the right person is of paramount importance.

Romance in the ancient world was a good bit different than it is today. In the ancient civilizations of the Middle East, Egypt, and parts of Europe, marriages were arranged by the bride's and groom's family members. People in these societies viewed marriage simply as an economic transaction—the combining of two estates—rather than as a romantic connection between the bride and groom. In these societies, the husband-wife relationship was first, one of duty, and second, one of romance, only if the couple were lucky. So young people in these societies prayed that the partner their parents chose for them turned out to be a romantic interest as well.

In some of these ancient civilizations, especially the matriarchal ones such as the Celtic tribes and the cultures of the early Middle East, romance that was lacking in the marriage could be found at the local temple in the form of hierodules (sacred lovers). The priestesses who served this function for the men of their societies are well known to modern historians. But what most people don't realize is that there were also priests who served as sacred lovers to the women of their communities. These priests were usually eunuchs in order to avoid pregnancy. Regardless of its form, romance was a powerful part of life for these ancient peoples.

Long ago, as today, romance was central to life—the fire and passion at the heart of existence. Spells and charms to win and keep love have been popular for age upon age. Use the following spells with discretion, respecting those you would bring into your life. Bear in mind that, while you can

Romance

draw love to you, you must never bind the will of another. To do so invokes the wrath of the gods.

Two Into One

The Greek deities Hermes and Aphrodite create a very special kind of magick through their union. They are two halves of a greater whole, uniting into the sacred Hermaphrodite (called after a combination of their two names). The two made into One then become Ouroboros, the Great Serpent that encircles and embodies all of Creation. This union is indeed powerful magick. In fact, the Hebrew and Arabic words for 'magic' are closely related to the words for 'serpent' in the same languages (Stone, 212). If you yearn for that special someone to make you complete, call Hermes and Aphrodite to your aid.

The Spell
What you will need:

- ✦ An unopened bottle of red wine.
- ✦ An unopened bottle of white wine.
- ✦ A wine glass of reasonable size (you will have to drink its entire contents during the spell).

Ancient Spellcraft

- ✦ A piece of gold ribbon or cord at least a foot long.
- ✦ A corkscrew.

Performing the spell:

This spell is best performed at dawn, preferably outdoors where you can see the Sun rising. The beginning of the day is a powerful time, very propitious for a spell that seeks a beginning for two people. Set all your supplies out together before you begin. Quiet your mind and open the two bottles of wine. As you open them, choose one to represent you and one to represent your true love. Call to the deities, that they may aid you in fulfilling your desires:

> "Hermes and Aphrodite, I call to You. You are two halves of the greater Whole, each incomplete without the other. I long for the completion of my other half. Please help me to find the right person to fill my heart and bring joy to my life."

Now stand the two bottles of wine next to each other. Tie the gold cord tightly around the neck of the bottle that represents you, knotting it so that it will not slip off. With the two bottles standing right next to each other, wrap the cord around the necks of both bottles in a figure-eight pattern—the symbol of infinity. Make sure the cord is loose enough to be slipped off the neck of the bottle that represents your romantic partner. You are calling this person to you, not binding them.

Now pick up the two bottles together, as if they were one, and pour the wine into the glass from both bottles at the same time. You are pouring equal amounts of red wine and white wine together. Watch as the two liquids mingle together, forming a new color, a new wine, just as two people who join together in love create something new—the soul of the relationship—by their union. Raise the full glass and say:

> "I call my true love to me. Whoever you are, if it be your will also, may we be united in love with the blessing of Hermes and Aphrodite."

Drink the wine slowly, savoring each taste. As you enjoy the wine, contemplate the concept of completion—the magickal union of two people into something much greater than either of them alone. When you have finished the wine, cork the bottles, but leave the cord wrapped around them. Save the rest of the wine to drink with the special person who will soon enter your life.

On the Wings of Love

Cupid was the Roman god of erotic love, the son of Venus and Mercury. To the Greeks, Venus and Mercury were Aphrodite and Hermes, who joined to create the perfect male/female union. So Cupid is representative of this perfect hermaphroditic union. Renaissance artists downplayed Cupid's real power and romanticized him as a chubby baby with little angel wings. But Cupid is a powerful god, not a cute decoration for a Victorian greeting card.

The Romans didn't make images of Cupid. There are no statues or paintings of him. Instead, they made talismans that represented Cupid's powers to bring love to them. Cupid's talisman inevitably took the form of a small phallus with wings. Such charms were commonly sold throughout the Roman Empire. In this spell, you will make your own version of Cupid's charm. Even though Cupid's charm is in phallic form, both men and women can use it to draw love into their lives.

The Spell

What you will need:

- An index card or other small piece of stiff paper.
- A dowel or stick 1 to 2 inches long. A toothpick is not thick enough to produce the desired visual effect. If you are feeling ambitious, you can carve the dowel into a realistic phallus shape. But a plain dowel will work just fine, too.
- Glue, scissors, and a pen.

Performing the spell:

Gather all your supplies together. Quiet your mind and concentrate on your purpose—bringing love into your life. Draw a small pair of wings on the index card. Make them small enough (about 2 inches wide) so that you can easily carry the charm in your pocket or purse. Cut out the wings, leaving them together in one piece, connected in the center. Glue the dowel in the middle, between the two wings. When the glue is dry, call on Cupid to aid you in your quest for love by writing the following on the wings:

Cupid of hearts

Bring love to me

By your ancient arts

Fulfilled I will be

Wrap the talisman in paper so it will not be damaged. Carry it in your pocket or purse all the time so Cupid's magick can work to transform your life.

Call on the Lady

The Etruscan goddess of love is Turan, whose name simply means 'the Lady.' Like many other ancient cultures, the

Etruscans believed the heart was the body's soul-center, as well as the seat of strong romantic feelings. They used the apple to represent the heart, both literally because it is about the same size and shape as a human heart, and figuratively because the fruit is sacred to the Goddess who brings love and life into the world.

Early Etruscan shrines were located in caves that were symbolic of the womb, which is sacred to the Goddess. Later in their history, when the Etruscans built temples as places of worship, they included underground chambers to simulate the earlier sacred caves. In this spell, you will create your own sacred cave. You will enter the Goddess's womb and present your heart to Her, asking that She find the mate for it, to bring love into your life. As always, remember that you are letting the Goddess judge who is the right person for you. Trust in Her and She will fulfill your dreams.

The Spell

What you will need:

- ✦ An underground chamber. This can be a real cave, but please be wise and enter only if you know the cave is safe, and never go alone. You can also

use any underground room—a basement or root cellar, for instance—as long as it is largely below ground level.
+ Two apples, one to represent you and one to represent your romantic partner-to-be.
+ A table or other horizontal surface in the underground chamber that will serve as an altar. It should be bare except for the apples you put on it.

Performing the spell:

This spell is performed over the course of three nights, preferably ending on the night of the full Moon. On the first night, quiet your mind and take the apple that represents you into the underground chamber. Hold the apple in your hands and call on the Goddess:

"Holy Turan, Lady of Love, I humbly ask Your aid. My heart is alone in life. Please bring love to me so my heart will not be alone."

Set the apple on the bare altar. Take several minutes to look at it and meditate on your aloneness.

On the second night, again quiet your mind, and this time take the second apple, the one that represents your romantic partner, down into the underground chamber. Hold it in your hands and again call on the Goddess:

"Holy Turan, Lady of Love, I know there is a heart that longs to share life and love with mine. I humbly ask You, please bring this love into my life so my heart will not be alone."

Put the second apple on the table next to the first one. Take several minutes to look at the two apples, next to each other, and meditate on the fact that there is a romantic partner for you. Avoid the tendency to go through the list of people you know and pick out likely candidates. Instead, trust that the Goddess knows who is the right partner for you.

On the third night, quiet your mind and go down to the underground chamber. Take a few moments to look at the two apples together. Think about what it feels like to be happy and in love. Believe that the right romantic partner is on the way into your life. Take the two apples in your hands and call on the Goddess:

"Holy Turan, Lady of Love, I thank You for Your aid. Thank You for the blessing of love that is about to enter my life."

Eat both apples, taking the spell's promise of love into your body and making it a part of your very being. Be confident that a new love, the right person for you, will enter your life very soon.

Paint Some Love in Your Life

The ancient Egyptians revered the ankh as the symbol of life, but its meaning is actually more complex than that. The ankh is a combination of an oval and a cross, two ancient shapes symbolizing the female (oval) and male (cross). Though we usually think of the ankh as a solid color, the Egyptians sometimes drew it with the oval in red and the cross in white. The red represents the menstrual blood that the ancients believed to be the source of human life. The white represents the blazing light of the Sun, the divine male force that brought life into the world. The ankh, then, is the magickal-sacred combination of female and male that creates life. Use this spell to bring the completion of romantic partnership into your life.

Ancient Spellcraft

The Spell

What you will need:

- ✦ A large mirror. Your bathroom mirror is a good choice, but any large mirror will do.
- ✦ Red lipstick or poster paint.
- ✦ White shoe polish.

Performing the spell:

Gather your supplies. Stand in front of the mirror and quiet your mind. Picture in your mind the ankh that you will draw on the mirror. At the top is a loop in red representing the female. Beneath the loop is a cross in white representing the male. The two halves will join as you draw the ankh, bringing the energy of a partner into your life. If you are a woman, you will draw the loop of the ankh first with the red lipstick or poster paint. If you are a man, you will draw the cross first in the white shoe polish.

Look at your reflection in the mirror and realize that you are one half of the ankh's symbology. Draw the first part of the ankh in its appropriate color directly over the reflection of your face in the mirror. Meditate for a moment on the imbalance and lack of completion you see in the mirror. Now pick up the other color and visualize the other half of the ankh on the mirror, attached to the half you have already drawn. This second half represents your mate, the romantic partner who will soon enter your life.

Avoid picturing any particular person in your mind, but allow your thoughts to be open to the wonderful partner the gods have chosen for you. As you allow these thoughts to fill your mind, draw the other half of the ankh in its appropriate color. Meditate for a few minutes on the image and feeling of completion and balance. Leave the ankh on your mirror for 10 days. Every day for those 10 days, look at your reflection combined with the ankh and remember that there is indeed a partner for you. On the morning of the 11th day, clean the ankh off the mirror to seal the spell, confident that the gods will bring you a wonderful partner very soon.

Initiate Me Into Love

To the ancient Cretans, the goddess Ariadne was the guiding light and the doorway to love. A spinner by trade, she gave Theseus Her golden cord so that he could find his way out of the Labyrinth and into Her arms. The Labyrinth symbolizes a journey of initiation, a finding of oneself and facing one's fears in order to attain fulfillment. The Labyrinth is not a maze or puzzle. There is only one way in and one way out, like a squared-off spiral. Ariadne's thread that runs through the Labyrinth, allowing the traveler to find the way out again, is the thread of the traveler's fate.

The Cretans used to perform a ritualized dance called the Crane Dance. In the Crane Dance, the dancers moved in a spiral inward toward an altar and outward again, as if they were dancing through a Labyrinth. At the center, they faced the altar and their own connection with the divine, the goddess Ariadne. As they spiraled outward again, they brought that spark of the divine with them out into the world.

Ancient Spellcraft

Here is your chance to dance the Crane Dance, to walk the Labyrinth to the Goddess and bring Her promise of love back out into the world with you. Remember, in this spell you are calling love to you, not forcing any particular person to join you in love. Ariadne knows better than you do who will share the path of your life. You work the spell, then let Her work Her magick in your life.

The Spell

What you will need:

- ✦ A Labyrinth. You can create your Labyrinth either on paper or on the ground. If you draw a Labyrinth on paper, you will also need a small stone or other token that symbolizes you. You can mark a Labyrinth on the ground using rope (or a garden hose), or you can mark it in the dirt with a stick. If you make your Labyrinth on the ground, make sure it is large enough for you to walk through. As you create your Labyrinth, concentrate on the purpose of the spell and put that purpose into the work you do to make your Labyrinth.

- ✦ A ball of thread or yarn, preferably gold in color (metallic is especially symbolic). Place it at the center of the Labyrinth.

Performing the spell:

Create your Labyrinth and set the thread at its center. Stand at the outside of the Labyrinth, quiet your mind, and call to the Goddess:

"Ariadne, oh You who holds the thread of my fate in Your hands, I call to You. Walk with me through the

Romance

Labyrinth. Meet me in the center that You may touch my heart and open me to the love I seek."

Slowly walk the Labyrinth inward, toward the center. If you are using a Labyrinth drawn on paper, slowly move the stone along the path of the Labyrinth toward the center. As you move, chant the following:

"Ariadne, bright and fair,

Come to me from above.

Spin Your thread of silken fate

That I may now know love."

When you reach the center, close your eyes and touch the center of your chest (your heart) with your hand. Feel the golden blessing of Ariadne on you. Now turn and move outward, toward the outside of the Labyrinth, carrying the thread of love with you. You do not need to unwind it to find your way—there is only one way out, and you already know it. When you reach the place where you began, complete the spell:

"Where I have journeyed, I now know the way. I carry the thread of love in my own hands.

Ariadne, bright and fair,

All honor to Your name.

I thank You for Your golden gift

And bid You return whence You came."

You may disassemble the Labyrinth or leave it as a subject for contemplation. Others may use your Labyrinth for their own rituals and spellwork without disturbing the working of your spell. In fact, several people together can build a large Labyrinth on the ground with rope, stones, or any other material they find suitable. Then each person may perform the spell for him or herself. Each person who performs the spell should have his or her own ball of thread, since each person has their own path and their own destiny.

Like a Cherry

The cornel cherry (or cherry laurel) is a tree related to the American dogwood. The cornel cherry tree was sacred to the Goddess in a number of ancient cultures that occupied the eastern end of the Mediterranean. The Greeks and Babylonians, among others, revered the tree and its fruit, using them in their sacred rites. This is the tree that classical authors sometimes referred to as a laurel tree. It is not the same as the modern bay laurel tree from which we get bay leaves for seasoning food. But bay leaves can be used for incense, just as cornel cherry leaves were used in ancient times.

The cornel cherry makes small red fruits about the size of a modern cherry, with a hard pit in the center. Cornel cherries, like modern cherries, were associated with the Goddess and with love. Cherry-red is the color of love, the deep red color of moon-blood. Cherries carry a seed inside them like the seed of life that grows in a woman's womb. This is the original source of the slang term "cherry" to refer to a woman's virginity.

Greek priestesses strung cornel cherry pits on a cord, much like a modern Catholic or Buddhist rosary, to help them keep track of the number of repetitions of prayers and other sacred acts. They also used the leaves as temple incense. The Greek goddess Daphne is especially connected with the cornel cherry tree.

The Spell
What you will need:

- ✦ Originally, cornel cherry pits would have been used for this kind of spell. You can certainly save the pits from some cherries and drill holes in them so they can be strung on a cord. But wooden beads work just fine, too. They can be a natural wood color or cherry-red. You will need 15 beads.
- ✦ A cord to string the beads on. It needs to be long enough to go around your arm or leg, with extra string for tying. Red is a good color choice.
- ✦ Bay leaves and incense charcoal. If you do not already have bay leaves on your kitchen spice shelf, you can find them with the herbs and spices at your local grocery store. You will need 15 leaves.

Performing the spell:

Begin on the evening of the new moon. Quiet your mind. Light a piece of incense charcoal and place one bay leaf on it. Inhale the aroma as the smoke drifts up into the air. Take one bead and string it on the cord, saying:

"I call my true love to me. Goddess aid me in my quest."

Tie the cord around your arm or leg and do not untie it until the next evening, when you repeat the process and string another bead on the cord. Tie the cord to your left arm or leg if you seek a female lover, and to your right arm or leg if you seek a male lover. The left side of the body has long been considered the feminine side, and the right side, the masculine side.

On the second night, repeat the chant twice, once for each bead you have strung. Repeat the process every evening until the night of the full moon. Each evening, you will repeat the chant one time more than the previous evening—always one repetition for each bead. Repeat the whole process for the final time on the night of the full moon. Depending on how the moon cycle coincides with the solar calendar when you do this spell, it may take 14 or 15 days. If it only takes 14 days, simply discard the leftover bead and bay leaf, or save them to use later for another purpose. On the last night, you will repeat the chant 14 or 15 times. When you have done this, instead of tying the cord to your arm or leg, firmly knot the ends together to form a circle, the neverending shape of cosmic connection. You may leave the cord on your altar, wear it around your neck, or carry it in your pocket or purse.

Joyful Union

The union of male and female has long been recognized as the source, not only of life, but also of joy. To the ancient Egyptians, the union of the Water and the Sun in the form of the hermaphroditic deity Meri-Ra represented this joyful union. To symbolize both the divine union of the powerful elements and the very human union of man and woman, they drew a symbol called the *menat*. This symbol obviously represents the physical joining of male and female, but it has greater meaning as well. It is the joining of male and female that brings about new life, and it is this same joining that brings knowledge of the divine to us in physical form. The Egyptians celebrated this sacred union and used the *menat* to bring this energy into their lives. Use this spell to bring joyful energy into your life, too.

The Spell

What you will need:

- ✦ A small container of rainwater.
- ✦ A piece of parchment or, if available, real papyrus.
- ✦ A sunny day.

Performing the spell:

Look at the *menat* symbol above and practice drawing it on a piece of scrap paper until you are comfortable with it. It is not a very complex symbol, and your copy of it doesn't have to be perfect, it just needs to be good enough for you to recognize its meaning.

Now gather your supplies in a sunny spot and quiet your mind. Lay the piece of parchment out and let the sun warm it. Set the container of water in the sun as well. The sun charges the water, just as Meri-Ra combines the power of Water with the power of the Sun. Meditate for a few minutes on the idea of completion, of joyful union between man and woman. Now you will draw the *menat* on the parchment using your finger dipped in the sun-charged rainwater. If you are a woman, use your index finger, which represents the feminine. If you are a man, use your middle finger, which represents the masculine. Draw the *menat* on the parchment with the water, dampening the parchment only just enough to see the image clearly. When you are done, set the parchment in the sun to dry. The image will disappear, but its energy and meaning will remain. When the paper is completely dry, fold it up and carry it with you as an amulet to draw romance to you and bring about the joyful union that the *menat* promises.

The Deep Blue Sea

To the Greeks, He was Poseidon. To the Romans, He was Neptune. But regardless of His name, He was the lusty god of the ocean, ever armed with the trident that bespoke His desire for the goddess of the deep. She, too, had many names in many lands, but throughout the ancient world Her oldest name rang simple and true—Mari of the blue waves and white foam. As a triple goddess, She requires a god with three times the usual "equipment" to satisfy Her desire and love Her as She deserves. So the sea-god's trident appears, three distinct phallic symbols held aloft by a muscled arm, poised to penetrate the beckoning waters. Such desire and attraction powers the very tides, or so the ancients believed. Now you can touch that power and use it to bring romance into your life. The names may change, but the game is still the same, the age-old game of love.

The Spell

What you will need:

- ✦ A clear glass of seawater. If seawater is unavailable, mix one teaspoon of sea salt in a glass of good quality water (spring water or filtered water, for instance).
- ✦ Three pearls or pearl-like beads.
- ✦ A small trident that will fit in the glass of water. Plastic tridents sometimes appear in various guises at seafood restaurants or adorning tropical drinks. They can be found in craft shops as well. Failing these sources, you can twist together a simple trident shape from thin wire such as florist's wire (available in craft shops).

Performing the spell:

This is a recipe for a "love cocktail." The ancient attraction of male and female takes shape in the ocean's waters, the very element of emotion and especially of love. Gather your supplies and quiet your mind. Set the glass of seawater in front of you and drop the three pearls into it. Call to the Goddess:

"Mari of blue waters and white foam, I ask Your aid. May You clothe my life in the radiant garb of love. As You join in love with Your mate, so may I do with mine."

Now set the trident next to the glass and call to the God:

"Lusty trident-bearer of the wild ocean, I ask Your aid. May You pour out love into my life. As You join in love with Your mate, so may I do with mine."

Hold the trident over the glass with its triple point downward. Realize that you are about to perform the *hieros gamos*, the sacred marriage of Goddess and God that brings all things into existence. With this act, you turn the power of the universe itself to the purpose of bringing love into your life. Now plunge the trident into the seawater. Meditate on the completion you have created, the attraction of one person for another that rules the tides of our hearts. Set the glass where you will see it every day. Let it remain in that spot for three days. On the morning of the fourth day, reverently remove the trident and return the water to the earth. Know that the most powerful forces of all are working to bring love into your life.

While the word *romance* may be fairly new, the concept is as old as humankind. Each of us yearns for a partner with whom we can share our hopes and dreams, our innermost thoughts, and our deepest love. Sometimes, though, life can be lonely. Sometimes we wonder if that special person will ever appear. At these times we can turn to the deities who have been revered for ages, for their help and compassion. They, too, know love and they can help bring it into your life.

Chapter 5

 # Fertility

fertile: adj. "affording abundant possibilities for development; capable of breeding or reproducing; characterized by great resourcefulness of thought or imagination" (Webster's New Collegiate Dictionary, *420)*

With so many definitions, the word is fertile indeed! As you can see, fertility refers to much more than just reproduction. In fact, a number of the ancient cultures represented in these spells flourished in an area called the Fertile Crescent. The area around the Tigris and Euphrates Rivers in the Middle East was home to the Sumerians, Hittites, and Babylonians, among others. These two rivers provided life-giving water that turned the barren desert into fertile farmland. The abundant crops supported burgeoning populations, fecund herds of goats and sheep, and a flourishing culture fertile with arts, crafts, trade, and religion. So you see, fertility encompasses far more than just the ability to produce offspring. It extends to the world of green growing vegetation. It even extends to the work of our minds and hands, the fertile creativity that gives birth to finely wrought craft and inspired art. Fertility is all about the creative processes of life, the processes that power the world.

Work the spells and charms in this section to bring every kind of fertility into your life. Here you will find magick

Ancient Spellcraft

to help you conceive children, to increase the fertility of your pets and your garden, even to avert impotence. Do realize, though, that none of these spells is a substitute for proper birth control or medical care. The fertility spells aimed at making babies also work well to bring fertility to your many creative endeavors. Simply substitute words and visualizations of your artwork, writing, or other creative work for those relating to pregnancy. Add this magick to your life and find fertility in its many wondrous forms!

MAKING BABIES

When a couple wants to have children, the wait for pregnancy can be agonizing. Even modern medicine sometimes cannot provide an explanation or aid for those who have difficulty conceiving. For millennia women have called on the Goddess to help them conceive. With Her aid, pregnancy becomes possible and the cycle of life continues on. Use the spells in this section to call on the Goddess who birthed the world. Bring Her fertility to your life and fulfill your dreams.

Water in the Desert

The Sun goddess who ruled the Hittite city of Arinna was named Wurusemu. She lived in the desert where water has been revered for aeons as the literal wellspring of life and where the Sun is the most powerful presence in nature. The Hittites, like many other ancient peoples in the Middle East, saw the Sun as a divine feminine force, the source of all life. Later cultures envisioned the brighter Sun as masculine and the dimmer Moon as feminine, but the oldest civilizations on Earth called to the Sun as Goddess and Source of Life.

Fertility

Wurusemu was Herself the mother of many goddesses and gods, so She is a wonderfully fertile source of aid in your quest for pregnancy.

The Spell

What you will need:

- A wide bowl, small enough that you can comfortably drink its contents.
- Rainwater or water from a spring or well, enough to fill the bowl or cup. Use water directly from the Earth or sky, not from your tap.

Performing the spell:

This spell must be performed outdoors at midday on a sunny day. The water that sustains life will combine with the Sun to create a powerful fertility potion. Fill the bowl with the water and set it in front of you on the ground or on a table or altar. Quiet your mind. Shift the bowl until the Sun reflects directly on the water. It will look like the Sun is actually in the bowl. Call to Wurusemu:

"Fertile Wurusemu who rides high in the sky, I call to You. Oh Queen of Heaven and Earth, maker of the cedar lands, I beg You to pour Your power out into this water for my sake. Send me the life-giving power of the Sun so that new life may grow within me."

Now watch the Sun's reflection in the water. Envision yourself pregnant, your belly as round as the Sun in the bowl. Do not move the bowl. Continue to meditate and envision yourself pregnant as the Sun moves across the sky, until the Sun's reflection is no longer centered within the bowl. Once the Sun has moved, pick up the bowl and say:

"I drink the power of the Sun and the Water. As they beget life on Earth, so may this drink bring a new life within my belly."

Drink the water down to the last drop, silently thanking Wurusemu for Her gifts. When you are done, you may wish to leave the bowl out where you can see it, as a daily reminder of the power of life within you.

Have a Little Party

Everyone knows how to make babies, and Cybele's cult in the ancient Middle East celebrated that. Cybele was the Great Mother Goddess who was responsible for the reproduction of all living things. Orgiastic ceremonies in Her honor celebrated not just love and physical sexuality, but also the fact that sex brings babies into the world. Cybele's followers played music and danced in the wild woods as a prelude to making love in Her honor and in honor of the timeless, powerful magick that brings new life into this world.

Lions are sacred to Cybele. A pair of lions pulled her chariot and she is often pictured accompanied by lions.

Fertility

Lionesses are very prolific, bearing large litters of cubs. They are also caring and protective mothers. The two lions that pull Cybele's chariot are a mated pair—one male and one female—as a reminder of Cybele's power in fertility. The color red is also sacred to Cybele, usually displayed in the form of red wine and red flowers. The color red symbolizes blood, especially menstrual blood, revered by the ancients as the source of life. Let Cybele and Her lions help bring a new cub into your life. This particular spell involves both members of the couple who wish to be parents, in keeping with the practices of Cybele's ancient rites.

The Spell
What you will need:
- A red makeup pencil (lipliner, for example) or red body paint.
- Music to make love by (your favorite CDs, perhaps) and a portable way to play it, if you will be performing this spell outdoors.
- Two lion figurines or pictures.
- A cup of red wine.
- Red flowers.

Ancient Spellcraft

Performing the spell:

Cybele's followers performed Her rites in wild woodlands and mountains, but you may choose the bedroom for safety and privacy if you wish. If you prefer to do this spell outdoors, make sure you have permission to use the land you are on, and take care to ensure adequate privacy.

First, set up a small altar to Cybele. Any horizontal surface will do. Set the cup of wine in the center of the altar. Do not drink this wine—it is Cybele's refreshment, your gift to Her. Set the lions on either side of the cup and scatter the red flowers over the altar. Turn on the music and take a few moments to quiet your mind, concentrate on each other, and get into a romantic mood. Yes, a spell is work of a sort, but this is an enjoyable sacred act as well.

When you have removed your clothes, use the makeup pencil or body paint to draw Cybele's symbol on the woman's belly. The simplest version of Cybele's symbol is an equilateral triangle (that is, a triangle with all the sides the same length) with one point aimed directly downward. This downward-pointing triangle mimics the shape of the woman's pubic hair below. As you create Cybele's symbol, ask Her blessing on your union:

> "Holy Cybele, great Mother of the Gods, creative source of life, we humbly ask Your aid. Pour Your power on us. Help us to bring new life into this world, as we celebrate Your ancient rite and honor Your name."

Take plenty of time to make love, and don't worry if you smear Cybele's symbol a little bit. She'll understand. When you are done, pour out the wine onto the ground as an offering to Cybele. Silently thank Her for Her gifts of love, passion, and fertility. Leave the flowers for Her as well.

Take your remaining tools home. Set the lions and the empty cup out where you will see them daily, and don't put them away until you are sure you're pregnant.

Like a Lily

The lily is a lovely flower found naturally throughout the Mediterranean, from Spain eastward around the Mediterranean to the coast of Asia Minor and northern Africa. But it played an especially important role in Cretan religious life. The lily has long been associated with the Goddess as a reminder of Her beauty, abundance, and fertility. The lily represents the femininity of the Goddess both in her sexuality and in her maternal fertility.

The popular incense called dragon's blood is actually the resin of a small tree (Dracaena draco or Dracaena cinnabari) in the lily family. Dragon's blood was highly prized throughout the ancient world for its value as a red dye, medicinal herb, and magickal substance. The ancients believed that dragon's blood increased the power and efficacy of any spell they used it in.

Ancient Cretan women offered lilies to the goddess Ariadne, wore them on their clothing and jewelry, and even drew them on their faces with makeup or as tattoos. The prolific lilies that filled the fields and valleys of Crete every spring spoke of Ariadne's fertility and Her ability to bring new life into this world.

The Spell

What you will need:

- ✦ A big armful of lilies. Day lilies and tiger lilies are easy to grow in your yard, and are also readily

Ancient Spellcraft

available at florist shops. Choose your favorite color, and include a few seed cases in addition to the flowers, if possible.
+ Makeup pencils or body paint.
+ Dragon's blood incense. You may choose powdered resin (which must be burned on incense charcoal) or incense sticks or cones. The powdered resin is more historically accurate.

Performing the spell:

Cretan women offered lilies to Ariadne at outdoor shrines in the Cretan countryside and mountains. Choose an outdoor setting where no one will mind if you burn incense and leave flowers. Gather all your supplies at the place where you will make your offering. Cretan women traditionally went barefoot when making offerings to the Goddess in order to be closer in touch with the Earth, which is Her body and Her creation. Set the lilies in front of you on the ground. Light the incense and set it next to the lilies. Kneel in front of the flowers, quiet your mind, and call to the Goddess:

"Ariadne bright and fair, come to me in this Your wild home. Accept my gift to You, beautiful lilies of the field, that I may bring forth life from my belly just as new life bursts forth from the Earth, Your body, each Spring."

Gather the lilies in your arms. Smell their fragrance and feel their texture. Feel the energy of blooming, burgeoning life within them. Now place them on the ground as your offering, saying:

"Blooming lilies of the field for Ariadne, goddess of life and love."

Using the makeup pencils or body paint, draw a lily on yourself—your face, your hand, wherever you prefer—to seal the lilies' energy into you. Now gently inhale the smoke of the dragon's blood incense. Savor its scent and let it empower your spell. Meditate for a while on the feelings of life that Ariadne brings to you, then quietly leave your offering for the Goddess.

Changing Clothes

In ancient Rome, a woman who wanted to get pregnant performed a simple spell by putting on the maternity clothes of a woman who had many healthy children. Along with this magickal dressing up, the woman might have appealed to the goddess Juno Curitis, the ultimate mother-ancestress of the Roman tribes. In the early days of the Roman tribes, before Juno was given a consort, the many Roman clans each traced their descent from a grandmotherly tribal ancestress after whom the tribe was named. Juno Curitis was the ultimate ancestress of the tribal "grandmothers," envisioned as giving birth to the whole Roman population. Let Her powerful fertility aid you in your quest to build your own family.

Ancient Spellcraft

The Spell

What you will need:

- ✦ One maternity outfit, or at least a maternity top, borrowed from a woman who has had several healthy children. Preferably, the outfit should look very "pregnant," rather than being one of the sleeker contemporary maternity clothing designs.

Performing the spell:

This spell, though simple to perform, takes a whole day. Explain this spell to your family and friends beforehand so they can help you by commenting on your maternal appearance when they see you during the day. When you get up first thing in the morning, call to Juno Curitis:

"Mother Juno, ancestress of great multitudes, I call to You. Bless me with the gift of a growing child in my belly that I, too, may one day be an ancestress."

Put on the borrowed maternity clothes. As you go about your daily tasks, have your family and friends comment on your pregnant appearance and pat your belly. Have them act as if you are already pregnant, and do likewise yourself. At the end of the day, take off the maternity clothes and again call to Juno Curitis:

"Mother Juno, ancestress of great multitudes, hear my words. Though I take off these maternity clothes, I still willingly accept and ask for the burden the clothes represent. Mother Juno, give me reason to put these clothes on again, I pray."

Silently thank Juno for Her gifts.

Fertility

Elephants!

In ancient Egypt, elephants were seen as highly symbolic of sex, possibly due to the phallic connotation of their long trunks. Male and female elephants were (and still are) referred to as bull and cow, thus relating them to the ancient bovine cult of Hathor/Isis. Hathor and Isis, both complex goddesses, had a fertility aspect among their many powers. The imagery of these goddesses as cows includes their function as mothers of great herds, other deities and humans, as well as their power as the source of life sustaining, overflowing milk. This imagery transferred to the elephant as well, a herd animal that nurses its young just as the cow does.

In order to increase the fertility of everything from their wives, to their livestock, to their fields, Egyptian men dressed as women, impersonated elephants, and used lewd language with heavy sexual connotations. The Egyptians performed this rite in large groups in a bawdy, Carnivale-type atmosphere. If several couples wish to perform this

Ancient Spellcraft

spell together, they can egg each other on. But it works well with just one couple, too.

The Spell

What you will need:

- ✦ Women's clothing for the man to wear—the more feminine and frilly, the better. The clothing needs to be loose enough that he can stuff a pillow over his belly in order to look pregnant. Makeup and a wig are also useful accessories, if they are available.
- ✦ A pillow to stuff under the man's clothes so he looks pregnant.
- ✦ A sock or stocking, the longer the better. Stuff it loosely with crumpled paper. Tie two strings, each about a foot long, to the open edge of the top—one on either side. You can do this by gathering the material into a small bunch and knotting the string around it, or by cutting a small hole in the edge of the sock and tying the string through the hole. The two strings will be used to tie the "elephant's trunk" to the man's face.

Performing the spell:

The woman waits elsewhere while the man dresses up in women's clothes. He stuffs the pillow under his clothing so he looks pregnant. He carries the "elephant trunk" with him but does not put it on yet. The man presents himself to the woman, all dressed up and walking in an exaggerated "pregnant waddle." It is perfectly all right for either participant (or both) to laugh at any point during the spell. Laughter is magick, too. The man asks a series of questions, which the woman answers as follows:

He: How do I look to you?
She: Pregnant!
He: How do you think I got this way?
She: The usual way!
He: And who is best at "the usual way"?
She: The elephant!
He: Why?
She: Because of his long, long trunk!

The man puts on the elephant trunk and lumbers around like an elephant (remember, he's also dressed like a pregnant woman). He brandishes his trunk at the woman and makes lewd and suggestive comments regarding its uses. As he does this, he begins to undress. A slow striptease is appropriate here, though getting out of women's clothes may be difficult. Once the man is undressed, he says the following, trying not to laugh:

"The bull comes to claim his cow. The calving season will soon be upon us!"

The couple makes love joyously, with laughter in their hearts, knowing that laughter and love are the two sacred things that bring new life into the world.

FERTILITY OF GREEN GROWING THINGS

Making babies isn't the only kind of fertility there is. Fertility applies to everything that lives and grows, including plants. The spells in this section are about the fertility of green growing things—crops, your vegetable or herb garden, houseplants, even your lawn. Everything

Ancient Spellcraft

that reproduces or grows carries within it the energy of fertility. To the ancients, the success of their crops and the strength of their medicinal herbs were among life's necessities. Though most of us now rely on supermarkets rather than fields and gardens for our food, the world of green growing things still adds beauty as well as nutrition to our lives.

Opening the Crossroads

For many ancient cultures, Wintertime meant that the underworld deities were in charge. The ancients believed that, during wintertime, the gods of the underworld took all the life-stuff down to their domain. To them, that explained why nothing grows during the Winter. The Sumerians believed that their 12 gods of the crossroads carried the green growing things down to the underworld during winter. These gods performed duties similar to those of the later Greek goddess Hecate, whose domain was also the crossroads. The Sumerian crossroads gods were responsible for moving people along their life path and transporting souls between the underworld and the upperworld. They also took the Earth's life force down to the underworld in the Winter and brought it back up to the world again in the Spring.

The gods of the crossroads sealed up the Earth with the coming of Wintertime, keeping its life-giving energies inside, protected from terrible Wintertime weather. In order for the plants to grow again and spring to, well, Spring, these energies had to be loose in the land once more. This spell opens the crossroads, the place where the energy was sealed, allowing it to flow into your garden and provide abundance and fertility once again. The Sumerians originally performed

Fertility

this "opening of the crossroads" with a sword, but you can substitute a knife and still work an effective spell.

The Spell

What you will need:

- ✦ A large knife or, if you have one, a sword. This should be a ritual knife if you have one. Otherwise it should be a "good" knife, not one you would mind throwing away.
- ✦ A clear spot on the ground in or near your garden.

Performing the spell:

Perform this spell early in the Spring, after winter's snows have begun to melt and new, green growth buds on trees and plants. To bring fertile Springtime energy to your garden, take the knife and consecrate it to fertility, saying:

"As this blade is sharp for cutting, so may its purpose
be sharp and well-directed, to bring fertile life back
to the land."

Clear a space on the ground in your garden and mark a crossroads in the dirt with the knife. It's a good idea to loosen the dirt a bit and remove any rocks before you draw the crossroads, so the knife will penetrate the Earth more easily. Plunge the knife as deep as you can into the ground at the center of the crossroads. Call on the gods of the crossroads, saying:

> "I call to the 12 gods of the crossroads. Oh You who sealed the Earth in wintertime to protect the vital life force, I call to you now to release it. The time has come. Spring is here. Let life flow once again on the Earth. May the green growing things live in strength and abundance in their season."

With a flourish, remove the knife from the ground, thus releasing the connection with the underworld and allowing life to flow forth again into your garden.

Mother Ocean and the Moon-Bull

Ancient people saw blood as a life-giving liquid and believed that it could induce fertility, that is, bring about new life. In ancient Crete the Minotauros, the great Moon-Bull, was sacrificed yearly for the fertility of the island. The Moon-Bull's blood was mixed with herbs and seawater to make a sacred liquid. The ancient Cretans considered seawater to be a substitute or different kind of blood since it tastes salty, like blood does. In fact, the Cretans envisioned seawater as the blood of Mother Ocean. The seawater blood of the Goddess combined with the bull's blood of the God to make a highly potent fertility mixture.

This blood, herb, and seawater mixture was used to bless the crop fields and orchards, "fertilizing" them for great abundance. The sacred blood mixture was held to be so powerful as to be deadly to mere human beings. Only the Great Mother, the Earth itself, was strong enough to handle this powerful blessing. In order to keep from touching the holy

Fertility

mixture, the priestesses and priests who performed the blessing used an aspergan to dip in the liquid and sprinkle it on the fields. An aspergan is a long stick with "fingers" made of reed on the end, quite useful for sprinkling liquids.

In this spell you will make your own version of this ancient sacred fertility mixture. You will use its powerful energies to bring fertility to the green growing things in your life.

The Spell
What you will need:

- You can use seawater as a substitute for bull's blood in this spell. Please don't go asking your butcher for bull's blood—commercial beef comes from castrated steers, and you don't want that kind of energy in a fertility spell! Sea salt mixed in with rainwater works just as well as seawater, if you don't happen to live near the ocean. A pint of water is sufficient for this spell. If you use rainwater, add two teaspoons of sea salt to a pint of water.
- A clear glass jar or pitcher large enough to hold the pint of water. A canning jar will work well for this, but a glass canister or pitcher would be more decorative.
- A teaspoon of each of the following dried herbs: thyme (Thymus vulgaris), bay leaf (Laurus nobilis), and rosemary (Rosmarinus officinalis). The ancient Cretans were very familiar with these herbs, using them in magick as well as cooking. If you don't already have these in your kitchen, you can easily find them on the spice aisle of your local grocery store.

- ✦ A paintbrush or other similar tool that you can use to sprinkle the liquid with. If you are feeling ambitious you can make your own aspergan. Use a dowel or small stick, about a foot to a foot and a half long, for the handle. For the 'fingers' you'll need a dozen four-inch long pieces of basketry reed (available at craft shops) or stiff pieces of pine straw. Lay the 'fingers' lengthwise at the end of the handle, overlapping them with the handle by about an inch. Wrap string or yarn tightly around the fingers to hold them in place. Your finished aspergan will look like a rustic little broom.

Performing the spell:

Pour the seawater into the container and add the herbs, stirring well. Cover the container and set it in the Sun. Allow the herbs to steep for a day, keeping the container in the Sun as much as possible. Don't leave the container uncovered. If you do, some of the water will evaporate due to the heat of the Sun. After the seawater mixture has steeped for a day, consecrate it in preparation for using it in your garden. Bless the container of liquid, saying:

> "Salt water that is the life's blood of Mother Ocean, bless the green growing things with abundant life. As the Moon-Bull once gave His blood so that the crops would grow with vigor, now I consecrate this liquid to that same purpose, in the name of Mother Ocean and the Moon-Bull."

Using the paintbrush or aspergan, sprinkle the mixture onto your garden. Please don't water your plants with it. Too much salt will damage them. Just sprinkle a bit over

Fertility

them for the blessing of Mother Ocean and the Moon-Bull. Also, do not touch the liquid with your hands. It may not be deadly, as the ancients believed, but please show respect for its power by using the paintbrush or aspergan. If you have any of the liquid left over after you have blessed your garden, houseplants, lawn, and so forth, return it to the earth or cap it tightly and save it, perhaps to share with your friends in their gardens. If you do return it to the earth, be sure to pour it in an area away from plants because too much salt may damage your plants.

MALE FERTILITY AND VIRILITY

While women have long called to the Goddess for Her aid in their fertility, for ages men have called to the God for His help with their virility. Virility is of course necessary in order for a man to become a father, but a man's libido is also a powerful part of his self-image. The virile gods of the ancient world offer their powerful masculinity in the following spells to avert impotence and assure libido. Of course, it is also prudent to seek professional medical advice for any physical symptoms you may be experiencing.

Like Water From a Spring

This Hittite spell to avert impotence calls on Hatti, the god of weather and especially rain and springs. The Hittites are named after this fertility god whose fructifying water brought life to the desert where his people lived. They offered grain to Hatti at shrines throughout the land in thanks for His gifts of water in its many forms. Without Hatti's gift of water, the grain would not grow and the people would starve. Hatti is often represented with his arms raised and water pouring out from his palms.

The mechanism in this spell is the metaphor of water spurting from an underground spring for semen spurting from the man—a form of sympathetic magick. The original version of this spell would have been performed at a spring or well. But even without these resources close at hand, you can bring Hatti to your aid.

The Spell

What you will need:

- A rubber balloon, preferably the kind that is designed to be used as a water balloon. Compared to a regular balloon, a water balloon is less likely to break when filled with water.
- Seeds. Choose whatever kind you like from the local garden store. The Hittites would probably have used barley or wheat, since these were their staple crops, but any kind of seeds will work.
- A bowl, if you will be performing this spell indoors.

Performing the spell:

Hatti's shrines were located outdoors where the weather could reach them, but you may perform this spell indoors if necessary. Gather your supplies together and quiet your mind. Call on Hatti as you begin, standing with your arms out to your sides, palms forward, in the gesture Hatti uses to pour water out on the Earth:

> "Divine Hatti, You pour out life-giving Water as a blessing on the Earth. Bless me, too, with the ability to pour out life-giving fluid, just as Your emanations bring life to the Earth."

If you are performing this spell indoors, place the seeds in the bowl. If you are performing it outdoors, sprinkle the seeds in a circle on the ground around you. Fill the balloon with water and hold it over the seeds. Squirt the water out of the balloon and onto the seeds. You may hold the balloon at crotch level for a stronger visual effect, if you like. When the balloon is empty, conclude the spell:

> "Fertile Hatti, I thank you for your gift of spurting, life-giving fluid. I ask that you give me always the ability to spurt my own life-giving fluid, in the same way that I have poured out Water on these seeds today."

As a gift to Hatti and the Earth, you may plant the well-watered seeds and watch them grow.

Those Symbolic Horns

The Minelathos, the great Moon-Stag of ancient Crete, is the royal animal who embodies male sexuality and vigor. The stag is the oldest known symbol of male deity, older than the ancient Cretan Minocapros (Moon-Goat) and Minotauros (Moon-Bull). As in the Greek myth of the goddess Artemis who turns Actaeon into a stag at midsummer to love and then hunt, the Minelathos is also a year-king. This institution is also familiar to us in the Celtic tradition as the Holly King/Oak King duality. In the Celtic

Ancient Spellcraft

tradition, the old king dies at midsummer to make way for the new one. The Cretan year-king, the Minelathos, also renews himself periodically, just as a healthy man finds renewed virility after each round of sexual activity.

Horned animals throughout ancient civilizations carry a double symbology. The horns are sacred to the Moon and hence the Goddess because they look like the crescent phases of the Moon. But horns are also a sign of virility, representing the libido and fertility of the male horned animal as well as the God. Horns represent phallic energy because they stand up long and hard. Kings in a number of ancient civilizations wore horns in order to show not only their divine connection with the Horned God, but also their virility and hence their ability to be wedded to the Earth in the form of the land they ruled.

The Spell

What you will need:

- ✦ Horns, of course. Bear in mind that you will be dipping the horns in wine that you will then drink, so be sure they are clean.
- ✦ A cup of red wine.

Performing the spell:

In this spell you will call on the Great Stag and bring His virility to you. Gather your supplies and quiet your mind. Take your shirt off. Call to the Great Stag:

"Hail Minelathos, great horned one, stag of the Moon. Come to me now, swift of foot, strong and sure, robust Lord. Show me Your woodland face."

Hold the horns up in front of yourself and admire them. Dip the horns in the cup of wine in an ancient gesture symbolizing sexual intercourse. Then use the wine-dampened horns to draw the shape of horns on your chest with the wine. Draw the power of the Great Stag into your body, saying:

"Hail Great Stag! Your virility awakens Goddess, Woman, and Earth to fertility and abundance. I drink Your virility into myself, draining the cup that you have blessed."

Drink the wine, then turn the cup upside down to show that it is empty. You have taken the Great Stag's power and vitality into yourself and are now blessed with his strength and virility.

Like a Palm Tree

The ithyphallic Egyptian god Min was always shown with an erection. He was a god of fertility, of course, but more than that, he was a god of libido and sexual ability. His symbol was a tall palm tree with two large stones on either side of it (yep, it looks like what you think it looks like). Ancient Egyptian men prayed to Min to help them achieve and maintain great virility.

Ancient Spellcraft

The Spell

What you will need:

- ✦ A toy palm tree, about 6 to 12 inches tall. Plastic palm trees are often available in toy stores, but if you cannot find one, a picture of similar size will do. If you use a picture, paste it to a piece of cardboard so it will stand up by itself. If it won't stand up by itself, you'll defeat the purpose of doing the spell in the first place.
- ✦ Two round rocks no larger than tennis balls.
- ✦ An altar or other space where you can leave Min's symbol undisturbed for a day.

Performing the spell:

Gather your supplies at your altar and quiet your mind. Stand the palm tree up on the altar and place the two stones on either side of it. Contemplate the meaning of this image for a minute or two, then call to Min:

"Holy Min who stands tall and hard, I call to You. I see Your symbol in front of me. Grant that I may achieve erections like Your palm tree, ever virile and strong."

Leave Min's symbol on your altar until the same time the next day. As a solar-oriented god, Min's works take a day to complete, one day being the smallest natural unit of solar time. You may choose to leave Min's symbol on your altar for an extended period of time as a reminder of His magick and power.

From the time the very first baby was born long, long ago, people have valued fertility and worried when it appeared to be lacking. Everything that lives and grows has a hand in fertility—people, animals, plants, even our creative endeavors. The blossoming of creative energy brings life to the universe. When you feel that your path of fertility is blocked, for whatever reason, call on the deities of the ancient world to help you achieve your goals. They brought vibrant life and fertility to these many ancient civilizations and they can do the same for you, too.

CHAPTER 6

protection: n. "supervision or support of one that is smaller and weaker" (Webster's New Collegiate Dictionary, 919)

Protection

Just as we protect those smaller and weaker than ourselves, (children and pets, for instance) so we ask the deities to protect us. The word *protect* comes from the Latin roots *pro-* meaning 'in front' and *tegere* meaning 'to cover.' In other words, to protect means to be a shield between the protected one and danger. The word *protect* comes from an Indo-European root (*(s)teg-*) that led to the modern English words *thatch* (that covers and protects a roof), *deck* (that covers and protects a floor or the lower parts of a ship), and the Latin *toga* (that covers and protects the body). For people of the ancient world, magickal protection was as vital an aspect of life as physical protection. They called to their deities for protection quite frequently and trusted that their spells would place a magickal shield between them and harm.

Please remember that protection is a defensive act, not an offensive one. Think of these spells as putting a covering (magickal armor or shield, perhaps) between the protected

Ancient Spellcraft

and harm. Bear in mind that harm can come from accident or random chaos as well as intent. The fact that something bad happens or threatens to happen does not necessarily mean that someone is out to get you. And even if someone does intend you harm, you do not have to do them harm in return in order to protect yourself. The spells in this chapter do not punish anyone for intending or causing harm. They just protect you and yours from harm, both intentional and accidental. Please leave punishment and karma to the gods.

Safety and protection are of paramount importance in a world full of dangers and uncertainties. Just as we are, the ancients were aware of the need for security in the ever-changing world. Protection from bad luck, disease, and ill-wishing ranks right along with safety during life's important events such as journeys and births. While the people of the ancient world may have blessed their cattle and carts, we can lay a spell of protection on our automobiles, pets, and computers, as well as on ourselves and our families. Of course, none of these spells can take the place of prudent real-world precautions and safeguards. There are more spells in this chapter than in any other chapter in this book because protection is of paramount importance. If we are not protected, we will have no chance to enjoy prosperity, fertility, and all the rest. This is indeed practical magick, a measure of added security to bolster our mundane safeguards in this unsure world.

Protection

PROTECTION OF HOME AND FAMILY

Of course, we must always take practical, mundane measures to ensure the safety of home and family. But we can add to those mundane measures with powerful spells. The spells in this section are designed to protect you, your family, and your home from random chaos as well as from those who actually intend harm. This includes people who purposely intend you harm as well as those who are simply combative or who may unwittingly cause you harm. Remember, protection is a defensive act, not an offensive one. The spells that follow are intended to prevent harm from coming to you and yours, not to do harm to anyone else.

A Magick Lightning Rod

The ancient Greeks believed eagles came from the Sun and were representative of all kinds of fire, including lightning. The Greeks placed images of eagles on the roof peaks

Ancient Spellcraft

of their temples in order to magickally deflect lightning, fire, and fire-based magick. This is the ancient ancestor of the familiar weather-cock seen on many barn roofs. The eagle certainly won't replace a lightning rod or a smoke detector, but it is added magickal assurance of safety for your home.

The Spell

What you will need:

- A picture of an eagle. The picture does not need to be very large, but it should be big enough that you can see it easily as you pass by it in your home. You can also use an eagle statue or carving. Just be sure that the eagle you choose will fit wherever you intend to place it in your home.

Performing the spell:

Choose the spot where your eagle will sit to guard your house. Over the front door is an ancient location for protective talismans, but anywhere around an entrance is a good choice. If your eagle image is not weatherproof, be sure to place it inside or at least under an overhang where it will stay dry in bad weather. First, bless your eagle to its purpose. Take it in your hands and say to it:

> "Sacred eagle, winged messenger of the Sun, I ask that you protect my home. Bird of Fire, please use your power to keep my home safe from Fire of every kind."

Carry the eagle all the way around your house three times to mark the boundary of protection and to seal in the eagle's power. Then hang or stand your eagle in the spot you have chosen. Every time you pass by it, remember that the eagle is doing you a favor by protecting your home, so nod your head to the eagle out of respect.

Brilliant Shining Truth

Apollo is the Greek god of truthfulness. He never utters any false word and in the ancient world his oracle at Delphi was renowned for always speaking truth. In Apollo's presence, no mortal may lie. Call on Apollo to protect you from deceit by always uncovering the truth. The Muses (and hence the number nine) are Apollo's sacred attendants and the laurel is also sacred to him. Use this spell in situations in which you believe someone is lying or may soon do so, especially if you believe they intend you harm. But bear in mind that Apollo's power works equally on everyone involved, and that includes you. So don't expect to be able to lie while others are required to tell the truth. Apollo requires total honesty from everyone.

The Spell

What you will need:

+ Nine bay leaves—preferably the Turkish kind that grow around the Mediterranean where Apollo comes from, rather than the California

Ancient Spellcraft

kind that aren't historically accurate and that also, incidentally, don't taste nearly as good when you use them in cooking.

✦ Incense charcoal, one piece for every day you will be performing this spell.

Performing the spell:

You may perform this spell for one, three, or nine days. Choose the duration of the spell according to the situation to which you want to bring honesty. If time is of the essence, perform the whole spell in one day. If the situation is ongoing or has not yet taken place, choose the three-day or nine-day version. Since Apollo is a Sun god, this spell is best performed at noon, when the Sun is at its high point in the sky. If you cannot perform the spell at noon, at least do it during daylight hours. Apollo is most powerful while the Sun is out. If at all possible, choose an outdoor location so you can see the Sun while you work the spell.

Gather your supplies and quiet your mind. Think about the situation to which you want to bring honesty. Reflect on the fact that Apollo will require honesty of everyone involved, including you. Light a piece of incense charcoal and wait for it to get hot. Pick up as many bay leaves as you will need for this day's portion of the spell. If you will be performing the whole spell in just one day, use all nine of the bay leaves. If you will be performing it over the course of three days, use three bay leaves. And if you will be performing it over the course of nine days, use just one bay leaf. Hold the bay leaves in your dominant hand and call to Apollo:

> "Arise, golden Apollo, like the Sun that shines golden in the blue sky. Shine on me with Your radiant truth, for in Your presence no mortal may speak falsehood."

Set the bay leaves on the hot charcoal and watch as they begin to smoke. Smell the fragrant smoke as it drifts up into the sky, toward Apollo's abode. Repeat the following chant three times for each bay leaf you burn:

"Apollo is with us. No mortal may lie."

Concentrate on honesty in the situation that concerns you, and meditate on it until the bay leaves have completely burned up and are no longer smoking. If you have chosen to perform this spell over the course of three or nine days, repeat the same process each day for the remainder of the spell.

Assistance With Arbitration

The goddess Aetna, daughter of Uranus and Ge, was the arbitrator between Hephaestos and Demeter when They quarreled over ownership of the island of Sicily, Aetna's home. She is the voice of reason who calls both sides to communicate freely and honestly. Aetna does not take sides, so don't expect Her to help you win a disagreement if you are in the wrong. But Aetna's energy brings fairness to disputes and allows reason and compromise to prevail.

Aetna gave Her name to a volcano on Her home island. Mt. Aetna is the tallest volcano in Europe and is still active. The ancients believed that the volcano erupted when Hephaestos (god of the forge and of volcanoes) argued with Demeter, the grain goddess on whose fields the volcano showered hot ashes and lava. The eruptions ceased, according to myth, when Aetna convinced the two deities to stop quarreling. Bear in mind that Aetna expects all disagreeing parties to compromise and listen to reason. So if you call on

Ancient Spellcraft

Her for help with a situation that you are involved in, She will expect you to compromise, too. Let Aetna help you douse the eruptions of discord and argument so everyone can reach a fair and agreeable compromise. Then carry Aetna's energy with you into the future, to avoid quarrels in the first place.

The Spell

What you will need:

- ✦ One cup of baking soda.
- ✦ One cup of vinegar (any kind).
- ✦ Two cups of water.
- ✦ A large bowl.
- ✦ A small bottle or jar with a tight-fitting lid.

Performing the spell:

Gather your supplies together in your kitchen or some other place that will not be damaged if you accidentally spill any of the ingredients. Quiet your mind. Picture in your mind the situation that is causing disagreement. Pick up the containers of baking soda and vinegar, one in each hand, and say the following:

"I put the dispute into these two substances. All disagreement and discord now reside in them."

Envision the disagreement within the baking soda and vinegar. Pour the two ingredients together into the bowl and watch them foam up like a volcano erupting as the two substances interact and "fight" with each other. Now pick up the water and call to Aetna:

"Holy Aetna, voice of reason, arbitrator to the gods, I call to You. Please bring Your power of communication and compromise to this situation, that reason may prevail."

Hold the container of water over the bubbling mass of baking soda and vinegar. Feel Aetna's cool, calm reason begin to influence the situation. Now pour the water over the baking soda/vinegar mixture. Watch as the water dilutes the other two substances and defuses the reaction. Feel all the disagreement cease as the mixture calms down and reason and compromise prevail. Once the mixture has stopped fizzing and is stable, place a small amount of it in the small bottle or jar and put the lid on tightly. This jar now contains Aetna's reason, Her sense of compromise and fair play. Know that She has brought peace to the situation that concerned you. Carry the small jar with you whenever you feel the need for divine arbitration and Aetna will bring calm and compromise to your aid.

A Shield of Protection

The Greek battle goddess Athena provides protection from one's enemies. She is often depicted with a spear and shield even though women did not carry arms in most of ancient Greece. Athena's power to protect and defend extends back to an age long before that of classical Greece, to a time when wisdom and protection were the domain of the Goddess. The memory of that age remained well into the time of classical Greece in the form of Athena's famous breastplate, the Aegis. On it was the image of the snake-haired woman referred to as the Medusa or Gorgon. This image was said to turn men to stone. But the snakes really represent female wisdom inherited from the Great Mother Goddess of long ago. This wisdom is the root of all protection, from a time when the clan mothers protected the whole clan as their children.

Athena's symbol, a triangle with a cross underneath it (pictured above), also reminds us of Athena's ancient wisdom and power. The triangle is a feminine symbol reminiscent of the shape of a woman's pubic mound. It is connected downward to the Earth, body of the Goddess, from which all wisdom comes. In this spell you will make your own charm in the form of Athena's breastplate. This charm is especially suited to protect women, but it will also work for men and children. Carry it with you or place it in your home to provide protection of all sorts, courtesy of the Wise Goddess.

The Spell

What you will need:

+ A small piece of cardboard, an index card or other stiff paper or board.

- ✦ Colored pencils.
- ✦ Scissors.

Performing the spell:

Gather your supplies and quiet your mind. Call to Athena:

> "Athena of the shining eyes, I call to You. Aid me as I make a badge of protection in Your honor. Watch over me and give power to my work."

Cut the cardboard into a circle no bigger than the size of your palm. On one side of the circle, draw Athena's symbol, the triangle with a cross below it. On the other side, draw Medusa's head—a woman's face with snakes for hair. Sometimes she is pictured with fangs or a vicious expression. This can be a very simple drawing. It does not need to be a work of art, but it does need to be recognizable *to you* as Medusa's face. Hold up the shield and consecrate it to its purpose:

> "Athena of the shining eyes, bless this shield with Your power of protection. As long as Your symbol shows on it, may it protect me in Your name."

You may place the shield on your altar or elsewhere in your home. You may also carry it in your pocket or purse, to have Athena's protection with you all the time.

Sacred Guardians

In ancient Crete, the Goddess was guarded by a pair of griffins. The griffin, a fantastic mythological creature, has the body of a lion and the head, claws, and wings of an eagle, two of the most predatory and aggressive animals in nature. The griffins flanked the Goddess, one on either side of her, as her sacred guardians. Because griffins represent the

Ancient Spellcraft

mythical aspect of Nature as well as reality, they guard in both the natural and supernatural realms.

The famous Throne Room in the palace at Knossos shows an example of the Goddess' sacred griffins. The throne, a large seat on a stepped platform, is the seat where the High Priestess reigned as the Goddess during rituals. On either side of the throne, painted on the frescoed wall, is a griffin under a palm tree, palms also being sacred to the Goddess on Crete. The Throne Room griffins are indeed powerful guardians, each standing as tall as a grown lion.

You may choose to use lions rather than griffins for this spell. Lions were also sacred guardians of the Cretan Goddess, but being real creatures rather than mythological ones, they can only guard on the physical realm, not the supernatural. Either way, these powerful sacred guardians will lend their watchfulness and protection to your life.

The Spell

What you will need:

- A photo of yourself or whomever you will be protecting with this spell.
- Two figurines or pictures of griffins.

Performing the spell:

Gather your supplies and quiet your mind. Hold the two griffins in your hands and call to the Goddess:

"Great Mother of All, I hold two of Your sacred guardians in my hands. Awaken them to their duty, I pray You, that they may protect me and mine."

To protect yourself or another person, place the photo of that person on your altar with a griffin on either side of it.

Protection

To protect your house, place a griffin on either side of your front door, on the inside or outside. If your griffins are not weatherproof, choose an indoor location for them. As you place the griffins in their guardian positions, remind them of their sacred task:

> "Griffins of the Goddess, guard well me and mine. With the Goddess's blessing, protect what is between you and me with all your might."

Every time you pass by the griffins, nod to them in respect, for they guard what is precious to you.

Footprints in the Sand

Pythagoras taught his students that a person's footprints are sacred and that harming a person's footprints would harm the person who made them. A number of other ancient cultures believed this as well. In our modern, paved-and-sodded world, we have few chances to make footprints. But this spell gives you that opportunity, as well as the opportunity to protect your footprints, and hence your whole self, from harm by others.

Ancient Spellcraft

The Spell

What you will need:

- A box big enough to set both feet in.
- Enough damp dirt or sand to fill the box.

Performing the spell:

Gather your supplies and quiet your mind. Fill the box with the damp dirt or sand. Smooth the top of the sand and look at it—clean and smooth, with no sign of you or anyone else on it. With your bare feet, make two footprints (one of each foot) in the sand. Now look at the sand. Your footprints, symbols of you, are clearly imprinted on it. Those footprints contain your energy. Acknowledge that your footprints are a part of you:

"I have made the imprint of my body in this sand. This imprint is part of me, just as surely as the path I walk is mine."

Now, with your hand, smooth away the footprints, saying:

"As I brush away these footprints, I destroy all means by which any other person might harm me."

Look at the sand now. It is as smooth and clean as it was before you made your footprints. Your imprint is gone, and with it the connection to you. No one can harm you because they can no longer get to your footprints. Let the dirt or sand sit out until it is dry before returning it to the place you got it from or using it elsewhere.

A Special Kind of Watchdog

The Hittite Goddess had a special guardian for her doorways. His name was Apulunas, meaning Guardian of

Protection

the Gates. His name is cognate to the later Greek Apollo. Apollo's regional name was Lycaeus, and he served the same purpose as the Goddess's dog-faced or wolf-faced door guardian. Archaeologists have found four altars dedicated to Apulunas in excavations in the area that is modern Turkey. In other words, Apulunas is the Hittites' sacred watchdog. Call on him to guard the doorway to your world—the front door of your home.

The Spell

What you will need:

- ✦ A dog collar, preferably black. This represents Apulunas, the sacred watchdog.
- ✦ Incense. Natural resin incenses such as myrrh, frankincense, and cinnabar are historically accurate, but any good incense will do.
- ✦ Dog treats (Milk Bones or something similar).

Performing the spell:

Choose a place by your front door for Apulunas' altar. It only needs to be big enough to hold the dog collar, but it does need to be reserved specially for Apulunas. You can't expect him to guard your doorway if you don't give him anywhere to sit.

Gather your supplies by your front door and quiet your mind. Light the incense and call to Apulunas:

"Apulunas, Watchdog of the Goddess, I call to you. I have made you a special place here by my door. Please come to this place and guard the doorway to my home. Let no harm or danger pass through this door. As you guard the Goddess, so too, shall you guard my home."

Place the dog collar on Apulunas' altar and leave him some dog treats. Periodically, offer him more dog treats so he knows that you appreciate his hard work.

PROTECTION FROM THEFT

Few acts confer such a feeling of violation as having one's possessions stolen. We must, of course, take commonsense precautions to safeguard our belongings, but we can also call on deities who specialize in protection from theft. Call on them to add extra security to your material world.

Hera's Statue

The Greek goddess Hera is the matriarch of the clan who resides on Mount Olympus. Her domain is hearth and home, and Her power is protection.

According to Greek legend, the priestess Admete took a sacred statue of the goddess Hera with her when she fled for safety to the island of Samos, off the southeast coast of Greece in the Aegean Sea. The rulers of Argos, where she had taken the statue from, hired mercenaries to go find it and bring it back. The temple where the statue stood had no front door so the mercenaries just walked in and took the statue. But when they tried to leave the island their boats wouldn't budge. Finally they gave up and left the statue on the beach. They also made a sacrifice to Hera, in case they had offended her by trying to remove her statue. Locals found the statue on the beach. Admete reconsecrated it and brought it back to the temple. The celebration of the return of Hera's statue became an annual festival on the seashore, complete with offerings to Her. In this spell you will consecrate your own statue of Hera and use it as a charm against theft. Hera's story is ancient and Her power is great. Use it to your advantage as long as you respect Her.

The Spell

What you will need:

- ✦ A small goddess figurine. It does not have to be specifically of Hera, but it definitely should not represent any other particular goddess. You can buy a small figurine or make one yourself out of modeling clay.
- ✦ Floral incense. Rose and jasmine are good choices, but any high-quality floral incense will work.

Performing the spell:

Choose a place for Hera's statue to "live." Gather your supplies at that place and quiet your mind. Light the incense and let the smoke fill the area where you intend to put the statue. Call to Hera:

"Great Hera, Mother of the gods, I consecrate this space to You. May Your spirit live here and protect my home as if it were Your temple."

As the incense burns, meditate on Hera's power and her ability to protect you as one of Her children. When the incense has burned completely out, set the statue in its place and announce:

"Hera is here. May She protect this house as if it were Her temple."

Once a month, burn more floral incense and let its smoke surround the statue to cleanse and recharge the protective energies Hera provides for you.

Ancient Spellcraft

Mind Your Own Business

Hermes protects from theft, especially in business, since thievery and commerce are both among His specialties. Before He was a day old, Hermes had stolen all of Apollo's herds. He gave them back, of course, but the precedent had already been set. Hermes is such an expert at theft that he can protect you from it. He is the god of commerce and business and is especially the protector of merchants. So call on him to avert shoplifting and commercial espionage. Take practical precautions as well, of course, but add Hermes' energy for the best results. In this spell you will make an antitheft charm, consecrated to Hermes, to help protect your place of business.

The Spell

What you will need:

- ✦ An index card.
- ✦ A pen.
- ✦ A small item that represents your business—a business card, company logo, etc.
- ✦ An envelope that the index card and business item will fit in. If the envelope is preprinted with your business letterhead, so much the better.

Performing the spell:

Gather your supplies at your place of business and quiet your mind. Lay all the items out on a table in front of you.

On the index card draw Hermes' symbol, a cross with a diagonal on top and an arc beneath (as seen on page 152). Hold the card in your dominant hand and call to Hermes:

"Hail Hermes, Lord of Souls, Thief and Protector from Thieves. Watch over my place of business and protect it from those who would take things from me."

Place the index card and the item that represents your business into the envelope. Seal the envelope and draw Hermes's symbol over the sealed flap. Place the envelope over the doorway to your place of business. If you can, balance it on top of the doorframe. Make sure it is secure and won't just fall off every time someone opens the door. This way, Hermes can alert you when someone who may intend to steal from you comes through the doorway. When this happens, the envelope will fall off the doorframe as the person walks through. Bear in mind, though, that having the envelope fall down is not cause for conviction of the person who came through the doorway. Just keep an eye on them for extra safety. If you cannot get the envelope to balance on the doorframe, you may tape it to the wall above the door. Either way, Hermes will protect your place of business from would-be thieves.

Protection for babies and children

The most innocent of all people, those new to this world, need protection the most because they cannot protect themselves. People have long called on the gods to help them provide safety and security for babies and children. Of course, along with protection of babies comes protection of the mother and baby during childbirth. Childbirth was about the most dangerous point in a woman's life in ancient times, so she called on whomever she could think of for help. With modern medical care, childbirth is not such a life-threatening situation, but it is still a psychologically stressful and anxious time for many. It is a time when the veil between the worlds grows thin as a new life comes into this world, so protection is warranted. Use the spells that follow to bring security, protection, and peace of mind to the momentous entry of a new life into this world.

The Safety of the Cave

According to Cretan mythology, the god Zagreus was born at midwinter to the goddess Rhea in her womb-cave on Mt. Dikte at the sacred center of the isle of Crete. Rhea hid the infant Zagreus in the cave for protection, giving him to the goat-goddess Amalthea to suckle. Amalthea's horns are the Horns of Plenty that provide nourishment and safety to babies everywhere, and Rhea's cave is the place of safe repose, a second womb of sorts, that gives safety from the dangers of the big, wide world.

Mt. Dikte was a sacred pilgrimage site throughout the history of Crete. Women would take their babies to the cave shrine on the mountain in order to receive Rhea's blessing on them. In modern times, we can journey to the Goddess' cave in our minds and craft a spell for the safety and protection of an infant or child. The child whose protection you seek may be present during the spellwork, but this spell works equally well for a distant subject.

The Spell
What you will need:
- A piece of parchment and a pen.
- An item to symbolize the cave. The cave can be symbolized by any container that can be closed to keep out light. A small, jewelry-sized box works well, as do small ceramic containers and little baskets. This spell refers to "the box," but you may substitute the name of the container you choose.
- A dark place in which to perform the spell. This spell is best cast at night or in a room with heavy drapes, the darkness symbolizing the security of the womb-cave.
- A photo of the child, if s/he is not present during the spell.

Performing the spell:

You do not need to make an offering during this ritual because protection and safety are every child's rights, given by the Goddess herself. In the quiet and dark, set the paper, pen, and box in front of you. Visualize yourself surrounded by the cave, its smooth, warm walls wrapping around you, above and below, cozy and warm, safe and secure. Call to the Goddess in whose cave you sit:

> "I call to You, Rhea, Great Mother of All. Your strength, Your wisdom, and Your deep faith bring us the knowledge of the womb-cave, the circle that holds all circles, everywhere and nowhere found, the Great Circle of Existence itself."

On the piece of paper, write the name of the child for whom you are casting this spell. Say the child's name out loud three times. If the child is not present, look at his or her photo and imagine the child to be present with you. Pick up the box and open it, ready to receive the child in safety. Ask the Goddess for the child's protection as you place the paper within the cave symbol, repeating the following three times:

> "[Child's name], I place you within the safety of the Goddess' cave. Great Mother Rhea, watch over [child's name] and keep him/her safe for s/he is one of Your children."

Close the cave symbol with the piece of paper inside, thus enclosing the child in the safety of the Goddess' womb-cave. Thank the Goddess for Her assistance:

> "I thank You, Great Mother Rhea, for Your strength, Your wisdom, and Your protection of this child. May You keep him/her safe until s/he is grown."

You may place the box on your altar or tuck it away in a closet or drawer. If the child for whom you performed the spell is not your own, you may give the box to the child's parent(s) or, if the child is older, to him or her directly. This is a permanent spell—it does not need to be turned off or undone, as Rhea's protection extends naturally until the time the child is grown and can protect him or herself. Likewise, opening the box or otherwise undoing the physical aspects of the spell will have no effect on the child's protection once the spell is complete.

The Warmth of the Hearth

The Roman goddess Vesta is the goddess of the hearth, home and family, and especially newborn babies who are

Protection

the newest members of the hearth. The Romans began and ended their meals with offerings and thanks to Vesta for home and family. Her priestesses, the Vestal Virgins, attended Her eternal sacred flame. Every home in Rome had the right to light their own hearth from this flame, since Vesta was the hearth made holy, the center of home life. Vesta's celestial hearth, the Pole Star, was considered the center of the universe since everything circled around it. The Romans called it the *focus*—the center of all things.

One of Vesta's functions was to protect all members of the hearth and home. Hence, it was most important to acknowledge a newborn baby as a member of the family as soon as possible after birth so that Vesta's protection would extend to the baby. The Romans acknowledged their newborns as part of the family by carrying them three times around the hearth while calling on Vesta to witness the event.

The Spell

What you will need:

- ✦ The baby to be protected.
- ✦ As many family members as are able to attend.
- ✦ A candle or oil lamp.

✦ A hearth or suitable substitute. Roman houses had freestanding cooking hearths in the center of the room where people could walk around them. But most modern houses that have fireplaces are built so that no one can walk around the fireplace. If you have a freestanding fireplace, by all means use it. But otherwise, you may use a table to make a family altar as a suitable hearth substitute. Set the candle or oil lamp on the table and add other items that represent your family such as photos and mementos. Creating the altar can be a whole-family affair.

Performing the spell:

Perform this spell as soon as possible after the baby is born. Gather the family around, create your family hearth-altar and set the candle or oil lamp on it. The baby's mother, as Vesta's representative within the family, calls on the Goddess while lighting the candle or lamp:

"Vesta, goddess of hearth and home, we light Your flame on our hearth and in our hearts. Come now and join us as we greet the newest member of our family."

Preferably, the baby's mother should carry it around the hearth. But if she is unable, the father or another family member may perform this duty. The baby's mother announces the baby's name, saying:

"[Name] is now a part of our family."

All the family members follow the mother as she walks around the altar three times, carrying the baby with her. While circling the altar, everyone present repeats:

"Welcome, [name]. You are a part of our family."

After everyone has gone round the altar three times, the baby's mother concludes the rite by saying:

"Vesta, we ask You to witness this baby's entrance into our family. We ask Your protection for him/her, who is now a part of our hearth."

A Favor From the Midwife

The Cretan goddess Eleithyia was the midwife-goddess, the protector of women during pregnancy and labor, and of babies through labor and at birth. Pregnant women from all over Crete traveled to Eleithyia's sacred cave Amnissos, near the great city of Knossos, to seek Her blessing on their pregnancy and Her aid in an easy birth. Inside the cave sat a large round stone with a hole in the middle of it, symbolic of the birth canal through which all people pass on their way into this life. Cretan women poured honey through the hole as an offering to the Goddess, to sweeten the time of their labor. Honey and, by extension, bees, were sacred to Eleithyia.

The Spell

What you will need:

- ✦ Honey.
- ✦ A stone with a hole in the middle of it. It doesn't need to be very big—the kind used in jewelry will do nicely, but be sure it is a real stone and not plastic.
- ✦ A container of sand large enough to set the hole-y stone in.
- ✦ You may also include poppy seeds in your offering, as they were also sacred to the Goddess,

especially for their calming and soothing effect on the laboring woman.

Performing the spell:

Set the stone in the middle of the container of sand. Put a dab of honey on your finger and taste it. Call to the Goddess:

"Eleithyia, midwife to goddesses and women, I taste the sweetness of Your presence. Watch over me and my unborn child; keep us both safe and sound as this baby grows large in my belly. I offer You golden honey, gift of the bees sacred to You. As the sweet honey pours through the hole in this stone, so may my sweet baby come swiftly and easily through birth and into this life. I ask this boon of You, Eleithyia, midwife to goddesses and women."

Pour the honey through the hole in the stone, filling up the hole to the brim. The honey will eventually soak into the sand, leaving a sweet film on the stone. You may sprinkle poppyseeds over the honey as well. Set the stone in its sand-filled container where you can look at it daily. Every time you look at it, recall the sweet taste of the honey and know that Eleithyia watches over you.

A Clean Sweep

Immediately after the birth of a child in ancient Greece, Hecate's priestess (who also served as the midwife during the birth) would sweep the threshold of the house to sweep away any evil spirits that might intend harm to the baby. In cultures around the world, sweeping has long been a powerful method of banishing negativity from an area. This is especially important right after a baby is born, since a newborn cannot protect itself and all sorts of stray energy is likely to linger after the hard work and emotional stress of childbirth. If the baby was born at a hospital, you may perform this spell in the hospital room. You may also perform it when the baby arrives home, providing a safe and magickal environment in which the new life can flourish.

The Spell

What you will need:

- ✦ A broom. It doesn't need to be a magickal broom—an ordinary household broom will do just fine. If you will be performing this ritual in the hospital, a small whisk broom will be less cumbersome and elicit fewer questions from hospital staff.

Performing the spell:

This spell is sublimely simple yet very effective. You may perform it with the baby in the room, or you may use this spell to prepare the baby's room before it comes home from the hospital. A female family member or friend should perform this spell, since it is the responsibility of the priestess, not the priest. Quiet your mind, pick up the broom, and call to Hecate:

"Ancient Hecate, Goddess of the Crossroads, hear my prayer. We have come to a crossroads in this family. A new life has entered the world. Please help me to make this place safe and loving so the new life can flourish."

Beginning at the door, sweep the air just above the floor all the way around the room. Swing the broom so that you sweep all the negativity out, away from the center of the room. When you reach the door again, thoroughly sweep the threshold. If you are performing this spell at the baby's home, first sweep the baby's room. Then sweep a path from the baby's room to the front door and thoroughly sweep that threshold as well.

Protection from Supernatural Sources

Just like the ancients, we of the modern world have access to many different practical means of protection in the mundane world—locks on our doors, hiding places for valuable objects, and so forth. But then as now, the mundane world offers little aid for protection against supernatural harm. For protection from harm that comes from psychic attack, harmful spells and other out-of-the-ordinary sources, we must turn to magick. Use the spells in this section to protect yourself and those you love from harm that comes from beyond the mundane realm.

The Writing Is on the . . . Stick

The ancient Irish Celtic Sun-god Ogma created ogham, a sacred form of writing used for divination, the sharing of arcane knowledge, and the working of spells. Ogham is traditionally written by carving it across the edge of a squared-off stick or stone. The sharp edge of the stick or stone becomes the central line of the writing (the 'druim'), with the symbols carved to the left or right of the druim or centrally across it. Each symbol has its own sacred meanings and is associated with a tree, a month, a deity, a color, and animals.

The ogham that confers protection from psychic attack and magick is Luis, written as two horizontal notches to the right of the center line. This ogham is sacred to the Irish goddess Brigid, since the month of Luis, from January 21 to February 17, includes her festival of Imbolg. Her tree, the rowan, falls within the symbology of Luis. In fact, in ancient Irish tradition, rowan groves provide magickal protection as well as earthly sanctuary to those within them. The color associated with Luis is "flame," the color of Brigid's inspirational fire, which offers additional protection from enchantment. As a triple goddess, Brigid is associated with numerous magickal triplets, and the number three is sacred to Her.

The Spell

What you will need:

- ✦ A piece of wood with a square edge, such as a 2x2 or a 2x4. It does not need to be very long (6 inches will do) but the square edge is necessary for writing the ogham. The piece of wood should be able to stand upright so that the square edge runs vertically.
- ✦ A small carving knife or permanent magic marker.
- ✦ A source of fire—a candle, fireplace, campfire, or cauldron. If you build a fire in a fireplace, campfire, or cauldron, add some rowan or mountain ash wood to the fire if any is available.
- ✦ A pencil.

Performing the spell:

Gather your supplies and quiet your mind. Light the fire and call to Brigid:

> "Hail Brigid, Three Blessed Ladies. Your flame of inspiration and protection reaches through all the worlds. Be with me now and bless this sacred symbol to my protection."

Take the piece of wood and stand it up so the square edge is vertical. Decide which edge you will use to create the ogham. If you choose to use a carving knife, carve two short horizontal lines of equal length to the right of the square edge on the wood. If you choose to use a marker, use it to draw a dark line the whole length of the square edge. Then draw the two horizontal lines to the right of the edge. Once you have created the ogham on the piece of wood, use the pencil to draw it (the vertical line plus the two horizontal lines) on the palm of your dominant hand. Pick up the block of wood in your dominant hand and hold it over the fire at a safe distance (this spell doesn't include a burnt offering!). Call to Brigid again, repeating the following three times:

> "Three Blessed Ladies, may Your sacred symbol protect me in this world and all others."

Silently thank Brigid for Her aid. Place the piece of wood where it will remind you of this protection. You may wash the ogham off the palm of your hand without removing any of the protection, because the magick is already in you.

Mistress of the Door

The Roman goddess Cardea is the door-hinge, the lover and consort of the god Janus, the door. Janus has two faces, one that looks back to the past and one that

Protection

looks forward to the future. From him we get the name of the month January that looks back at the old year and forward to the new one.

As the hinge of that magickal door, Cardea is the mover. She opens doors that are shut and shuts doors that are open. She is especially helpful in protecting people from the danger of ghosts and supernatural beings. In Rome she was offered pig's flesh and beans at her temples (perhaps the ancient predecessor to our cans of pork and beans?). To the Romans, beans were a sacred food, not to be eaten at ordinary meals. They were believed to be a favorite food of ghosts and the ancestors.

This simple spell is especially useful for protection from monsters under the bed and other supernatural concerns that may keep children from sound, safe sleep.

The Spell

What you will need:

+ Dried beans (kidney beans, pinto beans, navy beans, etc.).

Performing the spell:

There are two versions of this spell, both equally effective. If a child will be performing this spell and you use the first version, pay careful attention to be sure the child does not accidentally swallow or choke on the bean.

VERSION 1

Put a few beans in your hand and say, "I hold Cardea's sacred beans in my hand." Name whatever you are protecting yourself from (the monster under the bed, ill wishes from a neighbor, etc.). Put one bean in your mouth and spit it in the direction of what you just named. Do the same thing with two more beans (three in total). Finally, declare, "It is gone, thanks to Cardea!"

VERSION 2

At midnight, hold nine beans in your dominant hand. Loudly name whatever you are protecting yourself from and loudly ask it to leave. Throw one bean over your shoulder. Repeat the process (naming it, asking it to leave, throwing the bean over your shoulder) for the remaining eight beans. By the time you throw the last bean, the bother will be gone.

A Thorny Thicket

The blackthorn shrub and its Irish ogham character *straif* (related to the modern English word *strife*) can help protect you in both the visible and the invisible world. Ogham, an ancient Irish Celtic magickal writing system, uses simple sets of horizontal lines drawn to the left, right, or across the middle of an upright line (called the druim). The ogham symbol for the blackthorn is four lines drawn diagonally across the druim.

The blackthorn is a shrub that has long, nasty thorns. Blackthorn shrubs grow several together, into a thorny thicket. Its berries, called sloes, are made into an alcoholic beverage called sloe gin. Though used in modern times simply as a recreational beverage, sloe gin was originally a magickal concoction of great power and sanctity. The English word *slay* is related to the word sloe, so you can see the power of this plant against adversity, especially that of a magickal or supernatural nature. The blackthorn flowers during cold, nasty, wintry weather, so it is a great ally for finding strength and even beauty in the face of adversity.

Protection

The Spell

What you will need:

- Sloe gin.
- A thorny branch, preferably blackthorn, but any thorny plant will work (pyracantha, blackberry, rose).

Performing the spell:

Gather your supplies and quiet your mind. Pour a small glass of sloe gin. Pick up the thorny branch and feel how sharp it is, how hard it is to hold with all those thorns. Picture in your mind a huge thicket made of branches like this one, tightly interwoven so nothing could possibly get through. Anything that tried to get through would be torn to shreds just trying. Now picture this thorny thicket between you and the adversity you are protecting against. This is a magickal thicket—no matter where you move, no matter where the adversity moves, the thicket is always squarely between you and it.

Now dip your finger in the sloe gin and draw the ogham *straif* in the air where you envision the thorny thicket. Dip your finger a second time and draw the ogham on the palm of your dominant hand to seal the magick in you. Dip your finger a third time and taste the sloe gin, this powerful and ancient magickal potion. Know that you are protected by its great power. You may drink the sloe gin if you wish, or you may put it out as a gift to the Celtic Fairy folk who inhabit blackthorn thickets.

We protect those things we value—family, home, business. We put our energy into these valuable parts of our lives in the form of time, energy, money, and love, so we want to keep them from harm. Protection has been the uppermost concern of humankind for ages, for only when we are safe can we finally turn to the prospect of abundance, healing, and romance. In the modern world we have many means at our disposal for protecting ourselves, our families, our homes, and our businesses. But adding the protection of some of humankind's oldest and most powerful deities can lend a peace of mind that is not available from any other source.

Chapter 7

Healing

heal v. "to make sound or whole; to restore to health; to cause (an undesirable condition) to be overcome"

health n. "the condition of being sound in body, mind or spirit; flourishing condition: WELL-BEING" (Webster's New Collegiate Dictionary, 523)

Healing

When we talk about healing, even the dictionary definition reminds us that there is more to the process than just ridding the body of disease. The modern term *holistic* tells us that healing has many different components. It refers to the healing of the emotions and spirit as well as the body. In fact, the word *whole* is a close relative of the word *heal*. The modern English word *heal* comes from an Indo-European root (*kailo-*) that means 'whole, uninjured, of good omen.' Related words include hale, whole, wholesome, holy, and hallow (Watkins, 26). Healing is indeed a sacred, holy act of bringing mind, body, and spirit together in smoothly integrated, sound function. So you see, the family of words related to *heal* tells us what healing is really all about.

Of course we need healing for physical ailments such as disease and injury, but we also need it for emotional, psychological, and spiritual ills. Using the spells below, we can call powerful goddesses and gods to our aid for healing of all sorts. We can heal with help from deities, but we must also help ourselves. If I were to break my arm, I would first head straight for the emergency room, and then after receiving proper medical treatment, I would call on deity to help my body heal more quickly. Likewise, healing psychological or emotional trauma works better with assistance from an experienced clergy person or counselor. If you're asking for one kind of help, consider using all kinds of help available—conventional, alternative, spiritual—for faster, stronger healing of all facets of the complex being that you are.

In the modern world we tend to view medicine as a science separate from the other aspects of our lives. But the people of the ancient world felt that magick and medicine were inextricably bound to one another, and believed that medicine could not work without the proper magick to go along with it. Their local healer might offer herbs to help remedy an illness, but would insist on prayers and charms along with the herbs to increase their effectiveness. Here, then, is a collection of easy-to-do spells and charms to help you heal. These magickal workings are designed to be used along with proper medical care, to speed the healing of body and soul.

A New Beginning

Heather is a lovely light green plant that blooms a gorgeous purple on the cold, windswept heaths of the British Isles. In the ancient Irish magickal writing system known as ogham, the heather is symbolized by the letter *Ur*, written as three horizontal lines centered across a vertical line called the druim. The letter *Ur* means 'fresh and new', and is a metaphor for the morning dew. It is associated with the skylark as well.

Healing

Use this spell when illness is keeping you from moving on, perhaps a long or chronic illness that keeps you from doing what you want to in life. In this case, healing will mean a fresh start. This is also an excellent spell to use (along with professional help, of course) when you are coming out of depression.

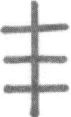

The Spell

What you will need:

- ✦ Morning dew, about a teaspoonful. It will take a good deal of time to collect a teaspoon of dew, but the energy you put into it will increase the power of your spell. If it takes more than one morning to collect a whole teaspoon, that's okay. Go out first thing in the morning and collect the dew in a small bottle or jar. Use a container with a lid so you don't accidentally spill the dew you have gone to so much trouble to collect. When you see a leaf with a drop of dew on it, hold the jar under the leaf and gently tap the leaf until the dew rolls off the leaf and into the jar. Collect the dew one drop at a time until you have about a teaspoonful.
- ✦ A soft (number 2) pencil. Make sure the point is fresh but not sharp.

Performing the spell:

These directions are written as if the person performing the spell is right-handed. If you are left-handed, simply reverse the hands as written in the directions below.

Ancient Spellcraft

Quiet your mind. Think about the illness that has kept you from moving on. Think of a simple symbol for the illness, perhaps the shape of the affected organ or body part. Now, holding the pencil in your right hand, draw the symbol on the palm of your left hand. Look at it, filling up your hand, unpleasant and ugly.

Now look at the letter Ur on the previous page. Think about what it symbolizes—a fresh start, a chance to move on after a long stagnation. Holding the pencil in your left hand, draw Ur in the palm of your right hand. Since you are using your off-hand to draw, you will find this more difficult than drawing the symbol of your illness. This is a representation of how it is more difficult and takes more energy and concentration to break the inertia and move out of illness than it does to stagnate and stay in the illness.

Now hold your two hands out in front of you and think about what each one symbolizes. Note that you hold the illness in your weak hand and the healing in your strong hand. Make the choice now to move out of the illness and into healing. State your choice out loud in a firm voice:

"I choose to move out of illness and into healing. I leave the illness behind as I move ahead on my life path."

Now pick up the bottle of dew, gathered with so much time and energy. You will now direct that energy into your healing. First, dip your finger into the dew and place a drop on your tongue. Taste its fresh coolness, the refreshing feeling of a new beginning. Now pour out half of the dew onto your left palm, onto the symbol of your illness. Using the fingers of your right hand, wipe the dew across the illness symbol until you have completely erased it. Wipe the dew

Healing

off your hand and look at the empty space where the illness was. Close your eyes and feel the empty space where the illness was. Now pour out the rest of the dew into your right hand, onto the letter Ur. Place your hands together, palms touching, and rub them together, saying:

"The illness leaves. I fill its empty space with healing. This is a new beginning."

Rub your hands together until the Ur symbol melts into the dew and is spread across both your hands. Do not wipe the dew off your hands, but rub them together until the dew absorbs into your skin. The healing is now within you.

Into the Abyss

Ancient Cretans called to the Goddess at cave shrines high up in the mountains of their island. These awe-inspiring nature sanctuaries were located in caves high in the craggy Cretan mountain range. The Cretans made difficult pilgrimages on foot to reach these shrines and ask the Goddess for Her aid in healing them.

Each shrine had its own particular deity and sacred festival, but all the cave shrines were ultimately sacred to the Great Mother Goddess Rhea. The tale of Her giving birth to the god Zagreus in a cave at midwinter is the oldest attested version of the story of the divine child born at midwinter. Caves were sacred to the Goddess as womb-symbols, reminders of the safety and healing of Her loving embrace.

To enlist Rhea's healing aid, the ancient Cretans would purchase a small charm in the shape of the body part they wished to heal. Numerous pottery and metal charms shaped like arms, legs, and torsos have been unearthed at the cave shrines on Crete. The Cretans then took their charms to the

Ancient Spellcraft

Goddess' shrines, asked Her assistance in healing, and threw the charms into the subterranean ponds and streams that flowed in the sacred caves. This practice is very similar to the modern Catholic practice of offering similar charms to the Virgin Mary (a modern face of the Goddess) at her shrines such as the one in Guadeloupe, Mexico.

The Spell

What you will need:

- ✦ Modeling clay, Sculpey, Fimo, or a similar substance. Play-Doh will do in a pinch. Choose a color that, to you, represents your illness or injury.
- ✦ A natural body of water (pond or lake) into which to throw the finished charm. Remember to get the owner's permission if the body of water is not on your property.

Performing the spell:

You may perform the entire spell at the site of the pond or stream you have chosen, or you may make your charm at home and then complete the spell at the edge of the body of water.

First, make the charm. Quiet your mind and focus your thoughts on the illness or injury you wish to heal. Choose a body part that represents the illness or injury to you. Mentally picture that body part, full of the illness or injury. Using the modeling clay, make a small figure in the shape of the body part. The charm should be small enough to fit easily in the palm of your hand. It doesn't need to be a work of art, but it should be close enough to the actual shape of the body part that you immediately think about that body part when you look at it. Now, take the charm to the body of water where you will complete the spell. Hold the charm in your hands, with your palms together, and call on the Goddess:

"Mother Rhea, You bring health and life to the world. I ask Your aid in healing me. Take this [illness or injury] from me, I pray You. I give it back to You. Swallow it up, Mother Rhea, so that it will not return to me."

Now feel the illness or injury in your body. Concentrate on that feeling. In your mind, picture the illness or injury moving out of your body and into the charm. When the illness or injury has moved entirely into the charm, open your hands. Take a deep breath and throw the charm into the water, shouting, "Be gone from me!" to release the illness or injury from your body. Silently thank Rhea for Her aid.

Healing Dreams

The Greek god Asclepius is the dying and reborn god, the healer of the ill because of his ability to bring about resurrection and hence, renewed health. His symbol is the double-serpent caduceus, familiar to us today as a symbol used by physicians to represent their practice. The two snakes that twine around the central staff of the caduceus are similar in symbolism to the kundalini/shakti forces that the Hindus believe flow up and down the spine in every healthy person. In ancient times, Asclepius's caduceus was topped with a solar/lunar disk bearing horns in the shape of snakes' heads. The imagery of the snake shedding its skin in rebirth reinforces Asclepius's ability to heal, to bring about a renewal of vigor and good health.

The rooster is sacred to Asclepius. Its crow heralds the rebirth of day, as Asclepius heralds the rebirth of life and

Ancient Spellcraft

health. This connection is symbolized by hen's eggs that have been dyed red, the color of life-giving blood. Asclepius is also symbolized by the Sun as it is reborn to power in the Spring.

Among Asclepius's underworld duties was the dispensation of sleep and dreams. In ancient Greece, those who were afflicted with illness would undergo a ritual purification and then sleep in the Asklepion, the healing temple of Asclepius. While asleep, the god would visit them with healing dreams, giving them new strength and vigor, and also blessing them with visions of things they should do to improve their health.

The Spell

What you will need:

- ✦ Six or more boiled eggs, dyed red.
- ✦ A quiet place, indoors or out, where you can lie down to receive the dreams. You need to be able to see the sunrise from this place.
- ✦ A blanket to lie on, if you're going to be outside.
- ✦ Incense. Sage, myrrh, and lavender are good choices for healing.
- ✦ Pen and paper.

Healing

Performing the spell:

You may begin this spell late at night or early in the morning before the sky begins to get light. Either way, the spell ends with the rising of the Sun.

Begin by bathing or showering to wash away the cares of the day and leave you pure and calm, open to the visions that will come to you. Set up the area where you will receive Asclepius's healing message. Lay out a blanket to lie on, if you'll be outside. Light the incense and allow its smoke to fill the area. Set the dyed eggs out in a circle around the place where you will sleep. By doing this, you surround yourself with Asclepius's power of rebirth and renewal. Sit in the center of the circle of eggs and call to Asclepius:

> "Asclepius, newborn god, Lord of the dawn, bring me healing visions as I sleep. You are the soul of health, the life in the growing day and year. Bring me strength and vitality. Awaken me to renewed health with the rising of the Sun."

Now lie down and close your eyes. Feel yourself surrounded by Asclepius' healing energy. Smell the sweet incense that floats around you and allow yourself to drift off to sleep. You will wake up when the Sun rises. When you awaken, sit up to face the rising Sun and again close your eyes. Breathe deeply of the morning air. Feel the renewing energy of the rising Sun as it shines on you. Recall the dreams and visions Asclepius sent to you as you slept. Think about how the visions can help you heal. Before you speak a single word or move from the circle of eggs, write down everything you recall from your dreams. When you are ready, silently thank Asclepius and put away all the items you used for this spell.

Ancient Spellcraft

You may not understand the healing dreams right away. Asclepius' followers often contemplated their dreams over the course of several days, sometimes even seeking the help of His priests to interpret the visions. You may wish to refer back to your notes over the next several days as insight, understanding, and healing come to you.

Teacher As Healer

Chiron, the wisest of the Centaurs, taught mankind about healing using nature's gifts (herbs, pure water, and so forth). The Centaurs were magickal creatures who lived in the wild mountains of Greece. They sported the bodies and four legs of wild horses, but had a man's torso and head where the horse's head would normally be. Unlike the other Centaurs who were wild and fierce, Chiron was gentle and wise. His kind presence among the other almost barbarous Centaurs is a reminder to us that Nature provides gentle sources of healing amid the ferocity that is the wide, wild world. Chiron also teaches us that ultimately, healing comes from finding peace within ourselves and not from any outside source. Chiron's wisdom was so famous that many prominent Greek heroes and legendary figures sent their sons to Chiron for fostering. He is immortalized in the night sky as a constellation that bears his name.

The Spell

What you will need:

- ✦ Fresh wild herbs. Dandelions from your lawn will do just fine, but if you have access to a field or forest, by all means, take advantage of the opportunity to explore and gather wild plants. You do not need to know what the herbs are since

Healing

you will not be eating them. NEVER ingest any plant that you have not positively identified as safe and edible. Also be sure you know what poison ivy and poison oak look like, and take care to avoid them.

✦ Fresh water. This can be filtered water from your house, bottled spring water, or rain water you have collected in a clean container. Please don't use water from a stream or pond, since you can't be sure it is safe to drink. Fill a clear bottle or glass with an amount that you can comfortably drink at once.

Performing the spell:

Choose a spot outdoors on a sunny day to perform this spell. If possible, go somewhere "uncivilized"—a forest, an abandoned field, or a mountain. Chiron lived in the wild and never strayed near any place that bore the mark of man. When you have chosen the place to perform the spell, make an altar area on a flat stone or a smooth spot of ground. Set the herbs and water on the altar. Quiet your mind and close your eyes. Picture Chiron's cave in front of you, dark but welcoming. He stands at the mouth of the cave, dark eyes gleaming, waiting to teach you his secrets of healing. Without opening your eyes, call to him:

> "Chiron, wisest of the Centaurs, I ask your aid. Help me find the source of healing in Nature and within myself."

Open your eyes and listen carefully to the sounds all around you. Pick up the herbs and hold them in your hands. Feel their life and power, an echo of the life and power of Nature that surrounds you. Lay the herbs out neatly on the altar and leave them there as an offering to Chiron.

Now pick up the water and hold it up to the Sun. Water is the basis of life on Earth and is an important ingredient in Chiron's healing techniques. Hold the water in both hands, close your eyes, and call to Chiron once more:

> "Centaur Chiron, gentle and wise, pour your healing into this water, that I may find renewed health and a closer connection with Nature."

Open your eyes and think about what is now in the water. Drink the water slowly, feeling the healing pour into your body. Silently thank Chiron and leave the herbs as an offering to him. Be very careful to remove any trash or other items you may have brought, so that you don't litter Chiron's wilderness.

Renewal Into Health

The labrys, or double ax, is probably the single most recognized sacred symbol from ancient Crete. Though often interpreted as a weapon, in Cretan ritual, the labrys served only a symbolic purpose—it represented the divine power of the Goddess in regeneration and renewal. The ritual

Healing

labryses that have been found at various archaeological sites, although beautifully crafted and decorated, are too flimsy and delicate to have been used for any practical purpose.

The labrys is, in fact, a stylized butterfly, a symbol of the regenerative and transformative power of the Goddess. She brings about renewal of life and health just as the caterpillar transforms magickally into the butterfly. This sacred tool also reflects the seasonal vegetative cycle the Cretans associated with the Goddess, for it is also shaped like the hoe axes the island inhabitants used to clear land for planting. So again the labrys symbolizes regeneration as seen in the seasonal renewal of plant life.

The goddess most closely associated with the labrys is Ariadne, who rules over initiations from one stage of life to another, and from illness into health. Use this spell to regenerate your health and transform your life.

The Spell

What you will need:

+ A labrys. It doesn't need to be very large; a piece of jewelry will do. If you don't already have a labrys in some form, you can draw one on a piece of posterboard. If you want to get fancy, you can paint it gold or cover it with aluminum foil so it looks more like the originals from ancient Crete.
+ A hand mirror.

Ancient Spellcraft

- ✦ A candle or small oil lamp.
- ✦ A makeup pencil or nontoxic Magic Marker.

Performing the spell:

You will need to perform this spell in a room that can be darkened and then made light again. During the daytime, use a room that has heavy drapes or blinds. At night, use a room with a bright light you can turn on and off. Gather your supplies, light the candle, and darken the room. Set the candle so that it lights your face from below. Quiet your mind, look at the labrys, and call to the Goddess:

> "Ariadne bright and fair, ruler of the changes in life, I call to You. Help me transform myself. Help me move out of sickness and into health."

Meditate on the process by which a caterpillar becomes a butterfly. The labrys in front of you is a symbol of the transformed butterfly. Right now you are the caterpillar. Pick up the mirror and look at your face, lit by the candle but surrounded by darkness. See the heaviness of illness in your face. See the darkness that surrounds you while you are ill. Now close your eyes and meditate on the caterpillar making a protective covering, a pupa, in which it can transform into the butterfly. Blow out the candle and experience the darkness cloaking you like a pupa, protecting you as you transform from the caterpillar to the butterfly, from illness to health. When you feel you have completed the transformation process, bring light to the room again. Now look at the labrys, the newborn butterfly, and look at your face once again in the mirror. Notice how different it is from the face you saw earlier. Look at the brightness that surrounds you, the light that reflects in your eyes. Feel yourself as the butterfly, your health renewed. Use the makeup pencil or

Magic Marker to draw a labrys somewhere on your body (on your hand or over your heart, for instance) in recognition of your transformation. Silently thank Ariadne for Her gift of healing and regeneration.

Trim Away Illness

A Roman cure for fever involved trimming your fingernails, mixing the trimmings with softened wax, and sticking the mixture to your neighbor's doorstep before sunrise. This procedure was said to transfer the illness to your neighbor. Of course, as much as we enjoy getting over an illness, we don't want to inflict it on anyone else. So rather than harming others, this spell has you remove the illness by burying your fingernail trimmings in the earth, preferably at a crossroads, which is the doorway to the underworld where illness originates.

The Spell

What you will need:

- Fingernail clippers or manicure scissors.
- A small container for the fingernail trimmings.
- Soft wax or modeling clay.
- A trowel or shovel.

Performing the spell:

Before you begin, choose the place where you will bury your fingernail trimmings. A crossroads is the ideal place, since the place where two roads cross is the gateway to the underworld. The underworld is the source of illness, according to the ancient Romans, and so the illness must go back to the underworld once it leaves you. If you cannot bury your nail trimmings at a real crossroads, you may make a symbolic crossroads by drawing a large X in the dirt with a stick or knife. Either way, you should bury the nail trimmings as close as possible to the center of the crossroads.

Trim your nails and carefully collect the trimmings in a container. Add enough soft wax or modeling clay to stick them together in a small ball. Hold the ball in your hands and feel the illness moving out of your body and into the ball of nail trimmings. Take as long as you need for this part. When you feel the illness has completely transferred into the ball of nail trimmings, take it to the crossroads. Using the trowel or shovel, break open the Earth to open the way to the underworld. Dig a hole and bury the ball of nail trimmings. Be sure to cover it completely and press all the dirt back down. This will seal the passage to the underworld so the illness cannot come back to plague you again.

The Hair of the Dog

The ancient Celts believed they could cure a cough by plucking a hair from the head of the cough-ridden person, laying it between two slices of buttered bread, and feeding it to a dog. They believed that, because dogs don't get coughs, this would not harm the animal and would rid the person of the cough. The Celts held their dogs in very high esteem and would not do anything to harm them. The Celts considered dogs to be the messengers of the underworld, able to travel with ease between that world and this one. Thus, they were capable of carrying illness back down to the underworld where it came from. If you have a cough and you also have a friendly dog available who wouldn't mind a little snack, this is the spell for you.

Healing

The Spell

What you will need:

- ✦ A dog. If it's not your dog, please check with the owner to be sure it's all right for the dog to eat bread and butter. Also, please tailor the size of the "sandwich" to the size of the dog. A Saint Bernard may happily wolf down two whole slices of bread, but a Chihuahua needs a smaller serving.
- ✦ Two pieces of bread, sized proportionally to the dog that will be eating them.
- ✦ Real butter. Margarine just won't do for this spell.

Performing the spell:

Butter both slices of bread liberally. Because this is a spell to relieve a cough, chances are you'll be coughing as you butter the bread. Every time you cough, feel the energy of the cough rise up from your chest, into your head, and into your hair. Once you feel the energy of the cough has saturated your hair, pluck out one hair from your head (ouch). Lay the hair on one slice of buttered bread. Lay the other slice on top so that you have a "hair and butter sandwich."

Feed the sandwich to the dog, secure in the knowledge that the dog will transfer the cough back to the underworld where it belongs. Don't forget to thank the dog.

Chill Out

A number of ancient societies used sympathetic magick to remedy illness and injury. They would transfer the illness or a particular symptom of it to an inanimate object. Fevers were of special concern because they were the main symptom of a wide variety of illnesses and could be quite frightening. Because fevers are hot, spells that involve cooling are useful for relieving them. By extension, similar spells will work for any "hot" symptom—arthritic joints, inflamed wounds, even hot flashes. The following spell is handy for these types of symptoms, but remember that no spell takes the place of proper medical care.

The Spell

What you will need:

- A smooth, round or oval stone. A polished stone that feels cool to the touch is the best choice.
- A bowl of cold water.

Performing the spell:

Hold the stone in your hand and feel its coolness. Imagine how it can cool anything it touches. Stroke the stone gently across the affected body part and feel the heat move out of your body and into the stone. For a fever, stroke the stone across your forehead and temples. For an inflamed joint, stroke the stone over the joint. Continue gently stroking the cool stone across the affected area until you feel that the heat from the symptom has transferred completely out of your body and into the stone.

Now that the heat has moved into the stone, you need to neutralize it so it won't return to your body. To do this, place the stone in a bowl of cold water so that the water completely covers the stone. For added cooling, you can set the bowl in the refrigerator. Leave the stone in the cold water for 24 hours to be sure the heat has dissipated and will not come back.

The Measure of Illness

In ancient Greece, those who were afflicted with illness took its measure and then gave this to a deity, asking that the deity remove the illness from them. Many ancient healing spells are listed as curing "fever," but this could mean any number of illnesses. The ancients' diagnostic skills were minimal, and many acute illnesses involve a fever. The Greeks would have taken their cord to the temple and offered it to a healing deity such as the goddess Hygeia, but you can perform this spell at home with a representation of the goddess. Hygeia's temples were often located near Asclepius's temples. The two deities were seen as counterparts, each bringing healing to humans in his or her own way. Hygeia's specialty is helping to heal the emotional as well as the physical aspects of illness. Her power helps break the despondency and apathy that can come with severe or prolonged illness. Use this spell to call on Hygeia so that She may help you heal body, mind, and spirit.

The Spell

What you will need:

- A statue or image of the goddess Hygeia, or any other deity who symbolizes healing to you.

Ancient Spellcraft

There is a great art nouveau print of Hygeia by Alphonse Mucha, often available as an inexpensive poster.
+ A long piece of cord or string.
+ Tape, soft wax, or some other method of sticking the cord to the deity figure.

Performing the spell:

Set up the statue or other image of Hygeia and stand in front of it as if you were in Her temple. Take the cord and use it to measure, in some way, the body part that is afflicted with illness. In other words, if you have a head cold, you might measure around your head. If you have arthritis in your hand, you might measure the length of your hand. Tie a knot in the cord to mark the distance of your measurement.

Using a small piece of tape or wax, attach the cord to the figure of the Goddess and ask her to take the illness away. Be sure to specifically name the illness or symptom as you call to Her:

"Blessed Hygeia, healer of the sick, please take this [illness/injury] from me. I give You its measure. Please free me from it."

Leave the string attached to the figurine. It will fall off when the illness has been totally released.

Getting the Point

The ancient Celts who lived in the British Isles had an interesting magickal method for helping a wound to heal. This quick and simple spell is for wounds caused by a sharp object such as a blade or thorn. Once again, sympathetic magick offers a way to augment our mundane efforts to help the body heal. Of course, please tend to your wound and provide appropriate first aid before beginning this spell.

The Spell

What you will need:
- The object that caused the wound.
- Soap, water, and a clean cloth.
- Vegetable oil—any kind will do.

Performing the spell:

Take the object that caused the wound and clean it very thoroughly, at least as well as you cleaned the actual wound. Once the object is clean, dry it well and oil it all over. Keep it well oiled until the wound is completely healed. This will keep the wound from festering and allow it to heal cleanly.

Sackcloth and Ashes

The ancient Romans celebrated the new year at the Spring Equinox, when life returned to the land and green things grew once again after the barren Winter. At this time they performed a ritual to "detoxify" their souls and their bodies, all at the same time, in order to remove the clinging illness of Winter and move on into a healthy Spring. They set aside their nice clothes and put on sackcloth—the simple, coarse woolen that slaves wore and that was used to make the sacks that held trade goods in the market. You might think of sackcloth as the ancient ancestor of our more recent flour sacks, which held flour as well as serving as the basis for clothing, quilts, and household goods. After exchanging their good clothes for sackcloth, the Romans then bathed in ashes or rubbed themselves with them to remove impurities in their bodies and souls. Because illness has a spiritual as well as a physical component, it is necessary to address both in order to heal.

Some translators have rendered this ritual as a way to expurgate sins, but the Romans didn't have the Christian view of sin and guilt. They did, however, know that bad attitudes, unhappiness, and general negativity can harm both body and soul and impede healing. The Romans used ashes in this rite because ashes come from fire, which cleanses and transforms everything it touches. Ashes burn away intangible, spiritual stuff just as surely as fire burns away tangible stuff. So use this spell when you need to detoxify your spirit in order to allow your body to heal.

The Spell

What you will need:

- Wood ashes from a fireplace, wood stove, or campfire. Please do not use ashes from charcoal briquettes.
- Plain, old clothes.

Performing the spell:

Begin by showering or bathing to remove all the physical and psychological debris from the outside world. When you have finished bathing, put on the old clothes. Don't wear makeup or jewelry and don't style your hair. This spell requires "just plain you." Now you have no pretense to hide behind—no glamour, no accessories. Therefore you cannot hide any negativity that needs to be released.

Quiet your mind and set the wood ashes in front of you. Think about the illness you are banishing. Feel the emotional as well as physical weight that it puts on you. Picture this weight, this negativity and illness in your body. Allow it all to flow through your body and out to your dominant hand. Feel all the weight of the illness in your dominant hand. Now take the index finger of your other hand and dip it in the ashes. Smear the ashes across the back of your dominant hand. Feel the ashes neutralizing the illness in your hand. The fire that created the ashes now destroys the illness, transforming it and releasing it from your body. When you feel that the illness has been totally released, wash the ashes off your hand to seal the spell and feel the new you.

Last Rites

The British Celts had a unique method for ridding themselves of an illness, especially one that lingered for a long time and refused to go away. They acted as if the illness had "died" and held an elaborate funeral for it, complete with a burial. This way, the illness was released from the person's body and returned to the Earth, "grounded out" so that it could not return. Use this spell to help release yourself from a stubborn illness that doesn't want to leave you alone.

Ancient Spellcraft

The Spell

What you will need:

- Several friends to act as "mourners."
- Items associated with the illness—thermometer, medicine bottle, written description of symptoms, etc.
- A box that all these items will fit in.
- A place where you can dig a hole and bury the box.

Performing the spell:

Gather your "mourners" and collect the illness-related items in the box. Everyone should weep and wail, speaking about the illness as if it were a dearly departed friend. Dig a hole big enough to hold the box and set the box beside the hole like a coffin beside a grave. Say a eulogy about the illness, talking about its symptoms, how it affected your life, and how your life is different now that it is gone. Lower the box into the hole. Have all the "mourners" throw a little dirt on the box before you finish burying it. As soon as the box is fully buried, everyone switches from sad and mourning to happy and joyful, congratulating you on your excellent health.

Healing comes in many different forms for the many different aspects of our lives. We can be injured on a physical, mental, emotional, or spiritual level and so it follows that healing occurs on all those levels as well. Since ancient times, magick has played a pivotal role in healing of all sorts. While modern medicine can heal the body and the psyche, magick brings healing into the spiritual realm as well. Of course, it would be foolish not to take advantage of all that modern medicine has to offer. But add to it the energy of the ancient world's deities and you have a truly powerful recipe for healing.

CHAPTER 8

divination: n. "the art or practice that seeks to foresee or foretell future events or discover hidden knowledge usu. by the interpretation of omens or by the aid of supernatural powers" (Webster's New Collegiate Dictionary, 331)

Diviniation

According to the dictionary definition, divination is a method of finding out things we can't ordinarily know. The term *divination* has a long and powerful history. It comes from the word *divine* meaning "of, relating to or proceeding directly from God or a god" (*Webster's*, 331). These words all go back to the Indo-European root *deiw-* which means 'to shine.' Not what you expected? This is the root of many of our deity terms in modern Indo-European languages. This single, simple root gave us the names of the Germanic gods Tiwy and Tyr, the English words deity and diva, the Sanskrit Devi and Devangari, the Roman Diana, Jupiter, and Jove, and the Greek Zeus. Interestingly enough, all these names really mean simply "deity" except for the name Diana, which can be translated "deity-grandmother" (Di-Ana). And they all refer back to the original root, reminding us of the brilliant radiance of the divine. It is this radiance that peeks through to us and glimmers enticingly as we briefly pull aside the veil and glimpse the future, the probable, and the hidden.

Ancient Spellcraft

The world is a mysterious place full of unknowns. Ancient peoples asked their gods for help and guidance, for information about the future so that life would be a little less uncertain. They used chants, charms, dreams, formulas, and tools of all sorts. They divined faraway and future knowledge in natural objects such as bones, water, and lightning, and in man-made objects such as carved stones. Of course, appropriate prayers and invocations to the deity involved are necessary in order for these divinations to work.

In this chapter you will find a number of simple, practical divinations from throughout the ancient world. Follow the easy steps and perhaps you, too, will catch a glimpse into the future. Bear in mind that what you see in divinations is only the probable course of events—nothing is written in stone. The information you receive in a divination allows you to make choices about your life path, and change the path if you so choose. You always have free will. The course of your life is in your hands.

Into Her Womb

Oracles in the ancient world were often located in caves symbolic of the Goddess' womb. Since all life comes from Her womb, secret and sacred information also comes from the same source. The oracle at Delphi in ancient Greece is one of the best known of the ancient oracles, located in a deep cave just outside the town. A similar oracle was located in a series of underground caverns outside the town of Gezer (18 miles northwest of Jerusalem) in Canaan.

Although the oracle at the town of Delphi, which means 'womb,' is often attributed to Apollo, it was originally dedicated to the Goddess in her serpent form, known as Pythia.

Diviniation

The goddess Pythia, represented by a python, gave mortals vital pieces of information through Her priestess, the Sybil. The tale of Apollo fighting the Python and winning is a legendary retelling of Apollo's priests taking over the Delphic oracle from the priestesses of the Goddess.

The oracle was given in a cave that symbolized the womb at Delphi by Pythia's priestesses who had inhaled the intoxicating smoke of dried laurel leaves (actually the cornel cherry). Bear in mind, ancient oracles didn't give set-in-stone predictions. The priestess counseled those who came to her for divination, giving them information on the best way to achieve their desired ends. Since human beings have free will, the future is not fixed, but the oracle offered information regarding what was most likely to happen in given circumstances. Prominent military and political figures consulted Pythia's priestesses when making important decisions. You, too, can call on the Goddess to find out more about your life path.

The Divination

What you will need:

- ✦ A cave-like setting. This can be an actual cave (please be sure it is safe) or a darkened room or large closet. You can even make a homemade "cave" by draping a blanket over a table.

Ancient Spellcraft

- Bay laurel leaves and incense charcoal to burn them on. The Delphic priestesses used cornel cherry leaves for their intoxicating incense. You can substitute the leaves of the closely related bay laurel tree, commonly available in the spice aisle of your local grocery store. Please choose Turkish bay leaves if they are available. They are much more pleasantly scented than the California variety, and they come from the same geographic region that Pythia's priestesses presided over.
- A candle or other small light source.
- A snake image such as a picture of a snake or a rubber snake. This represents the Goddess Pythia.

Performing the divination:

Spend some time thinking about the question you will ask of Pythia before you begin. Think about the areas of your life in which you must make decisions. Settle on a specific topic or situation to ask about, then create your cave space and assemble your supplies in it. Make a comfortable spot to sit in since the divination may take some time. Quiet your mind. Light the candle and the incense charcoal. Set the snake where you can see it out of the corner of your eye when you look at the candle. When the charcoal is hot, place three bay leaves on it. The number three is sacred to Pythia, whose priestesses sat on three-legged stools to pronounce their oracles. As the smoke from the burning bay leaves begins to rise into the air, watch the shapes it makes in the feeble light of the cave. Concentrate on the question you want to ask. When the question is clear in your mind, call to Pythia:

Diviniation

"Ancient Pythia who dwells in the cave, bless me with Your sacred serpent's wisdom."

Ask your question out loud. Now stare at the candle as its light flickers in the smoky cave. Allow your gaze to drift out of focus as various shapes move in and out of your field of vision. Allow yourself to see whatever Pythia presents to you. Do not rush this process; it takes time. Pythia will give you visions that answer your question and give you insight into the situation you asked about, but only if you let Her. If you wish, you may add three more bay leaves to the incense charcoal when the first three have stopped smoking. When you have seen all that Pythia has to show you, thank Her. Extinguish the candle and clean up after yourself. As you go about your daily routine for the next three days, reflect on the visions Pythia has shown you.

Where Will They Fall?

The Druids, who served as priests and advisors to the ancient Celtic chieftains, had a simple but very useful system of divination to see how people would react in a given situation. The Druids were political as well as spiritual advisors to the Celtic chieftains, and the chieftains often needed to know whether people would be with them or turn against them if they made certain decisions. Knowing how their people were likely to react in a given situation could help a chieftain make a wise and politically astute decision.

In modern life, we often find similar information useful as well. Knowing whether your co-workers are likely to support you, or scatter, or gang up against you when you present a new idea can be helpful in figuring out how to prepare your presentation.

Ancient Spellcraft

Bear in mind that this divination, like all others, simply shows you the most likely course of events given the current path. The Druids went through anywhere from 12 to 20 years of training in order to perform their sacred duties, so don't expect to see the detailed future of the whole world right off the bat. Stick with situations that directly involve you and pay attention to what you're doing, and the stones will tell you what you need to know.

The Divination

What you will need:

- Small rounded stones of similar size, one for every person involved in the situation you are asking about. The pebbles sold at home improvement stores for decorative landscaping work well and are inexpensive. The Druids used the stones they had at hand, not expensive stones fit for jewelry.
- A smooth patch of ground (no grass, please) or carpet on which to throw the stones. Don't use a hard surface such as a tabletop—the stones will roll around too much.

Performing the divination:

Choose one recognizable stone to represent yourself (maybe paint it or mark a dot on it). This works best for determining how groups of people will behave in a given situation, so don't mark every stone to represent a specific person. That's too much information for a simple divination to provide. But do choose a number of stones comparable to the number of people involved in the situation. Hold all the stones in your dominant hand and clearly focus your thoughts on the situation that you want information about. This could be a decision you are going to make or an action

Diviniation

you intend to take. Your thoughts should be in the form, "If I do such-and-such, how will the people around me react?"

When the thought is clear in your mind, close your eyes (if they're not closed already) and gently toss the stones onto the surface you have chosen. Open your eyes and see how the stones are arranged around the one that represents you. If all the stones are clustered around your stone, expect the people to support you in this situation. If only one or two stones are next to yours, expect only a few people to support you. If many of the stones are scattered widely, the people involved will likewise scatter and avoid involvement in the situation. If a number of the stones are clustered tightly together, but away from your stone, expect some of the people involved to gather together in opposition to you in this situation.

If you are trying to decide on a course of action to take in a given situation, it can be useful to do a separate throw for each possible path you might choose to take. See how the people around you are likely to react to your actions, and include that information in your decision-making process. This way you can determine how best to prepare yourself in order to be successful in the situation in question.

Seeing in a Storm

The Etruscan sky god Tin is shown as a young man with a thunderbolt in his right hand. He is responsible for all the weather emanating from the sky, especially thunderstorms. The Etruscans divined future and past information in patterns of lightning during thunderstorms. Of course, standing outside in a thunderstorm isn't particularly safe, but you can perform this divination safely from behind a large

Ancient Spellcraft

window. Just be sure to keep the window closed, and don't touch the window frame. You'll need to know which way the cardinal directions (north, south, east, and west) are oriented in order to read the omens. So take advantage of Nature's spectacular thunderstorm "shows," and call on Tin to help you find new information in the weather.

The Divination

What you will need:

- ✦ A thunderstorm. You can perform this divination any time of day or night, as long as the lightning is clearly visible in the sky.
- ✦ A compass or other accurate way to gauge the directions.
- ✦ Pen and paper to record the things you see.
- ✦ A window facing north. Keep the window closed and do not touch the window frame while the thunderstorm is active.

Performing the divination:

During a thunderstorm, face north and watch the lightning as it shimmers in the sky. Tin resides in the north and creates thunderstorms, so you can call to Him to help you read the information in the storm. Think of a situation in

Divination

your life about which you would like to find out more information. Concentrate on the situation and call to Tin:

"Mighty Tin of the north, ruler of the sky, I see Your power. Please aid me in my quest for knowledge today."

Now watch the sky to see where the lightning strikes. Make note of where the lightning strikes and whether it is weak or strong. Note single strikes and repeated strikes. When the storm has passed, compare your notes to the information here to glean valuable information about the situation that concerns you.

Lightning strikes in front of you indicate future events, those behind you indicate past events, and those directly overhead indicate events in current time. Lightning strikes to your left indicate good omens and to your right indicate bad omens. You can combine these meanings. For instance, a series of lightning strikes in front of you on the left side of the sky indicates a very positive future outlook for the situation in question. A number of lightning strikes in a row is a much stronger sign than a single lightning strike. Lightning that is far away is a weaker sign than lightning that strikes nearby.

The part of the sky the storm is in or comes from also has meaning. A storm in the east/northeast (in front of you on the right as you're facing out the window) indicates the influence of powerful supernatural forces, usually deities, in your life regarding the subject you're divining about. A thunderstorm in the west/northwest (in front of you on the left) indicates the influence of fate and the underworld, in other words, your destiny and hidden life path, regarding the subject you're divining about. A storm to the south indicates the influence of Earth, Nature, and natural forces.

Ancient Spellcraft

The Lottery

The Hittites used a lottery somewhat like our modern dominoes to divine unseen information. This system requires that the user carefully construct their questions, because the lottery can give only limited answers. This divination is designed using commonly-available modern dominoes. This is a very simple divination method that, when used with a little patience, can provide you with very useful information.

The Divination

What you will need:

- ✦ A set of dominoes. Inexpensive versions are available at toy stores and in the toy department of large discount and department stores.
- ✦ A box or bag to shake the dominoes in.
- ✦ A smooth, hard surface such as a floor or tabletop to toss the dominoes onto.

Performing the divination:

We do not have complete information about the Hittite lottery system of divination, so I have filled in the gaps where necessary and constructed an easy-to-use version of the complex ancient system. Modern dominoes have two numbers on each tile, one on each end. For this divination you will

Diviniation

use only the tiles that have the same number on both ends. Set aside all the tiles that contain two different numbers. Choose the domino that has two blanks on it (no numbers) to represent yourself. Put the blank domino and all the doubles into the box or bag. Quiet your mind. Formulate a question in your mind and shake the dominoes as you think about the question. The question should be in the form, "What will be the result if I do X?" When you are ready and the question is clear in your mind, gently toss the dominoes out onto the tabletop or floor. If any tiles land standing up on their side, you will need to reformulate your question and throw the tiles again. Upside-down tiles indicate forces that act negatively in this situation. Right-side-up tiles indicate positive influences. If the tile that represents you is upside down, the situation is negative or potentially dangerous for you.

Locate the tile that represents yourself and read the meaning of the other tiles in relation to it. Look at the tiles that have fallen around yours. The closer a tile is to yours, the stronger its influence on the situation. The farther away a tile is from yours, the weaker its influence. If one tile covers or lies on top of another, this means that the one on top is covering up or obscuring the influence of the one underneath. If a tile lies partly or totally on top of yours, this means that influence is hindering or blocking you in the situation you asked about. The basic meanings of the tiles are:

1. Religion, deity, the supernatural.
2. Immediate family, home.
3. Friends, co-workers, and extended family.
4. Leisure, arts, creative activities, imagination.
5. Work and business-related matters, finances.
6. Health-related matters.

Ancient Spellcraft

You can refine the information you get by asking further questions and tossing the dominoes again.

You can also use the tiles to answer yes/no questions in order to clarify your divination. Simply choose any five tiles at random. Hold them in your hand and clearly formulate the question in your mind. Toss the tiles onto the tabletop. Right-side-up tiles indicate yes and upside-down tiles indicate no. Read the answer according to the way the majority of the tiles are turned. All five tiles turned the same way is an unequivocal answer. Four of the five tiles turned the same way is a strong answer. Three of the five tiles turned the same way indicate a weak answer. In this last case you should reformulate your question and throw the tiles again for a clearer answer.

The Face of Your Child-to-Be

Pregnant women in ancient Crete journeyed to the cave Amnisos, sacred to the midwife-goddess Eleithyia. There they asked Her aid in a safe and easy labor and sought visions of the faces of their soon-to-be-born children. In the darkness of the cave, the women sat among stalagmites, giant pillars of stone built up slowly over the eons as the water slowly dripped from the ceiling of the cave. Three of these pillars naturally formed the shapes of an old woman, a pregnant woman, and a child—the ancient sacred trinity of childbirth. In this trio the old woman represents the crone/midwife. At the base of each pillar glimmered a pool of water, a scrying pool into which the woman could peer in, seeking her visions. Upon entering the cave, each woman made an offering of honey to the Goddess before gazing into the pools of water. Journey to Eleithyia's cave yourself to glimpse the beautiful face of the baby who will soon enter your life.

The Divination

What you will need:

- ✦ Three bowls made of a dark material, similar in size and shape, filled with water.
- ✦ Honey.
- ✦ Small dish for the honey offering.
- ✦ (Optional) Figurines of crone, pregnant woman, and baby or child.

Performing the divination:

This is best done outside at night, with moon and starlight to reflect off the surface of the water. If weather restricts you to the indoors, a dark room with a gentle, indirect source of light (a candle or dim lamp) will work, too. Since this is a divination done by a pregnant woman, be sure to arrange the scrying bowls and your seating in such a way that you will be comfortable sitting in the same place for a while.

Place the bowls of water in a row in front of you. If you like, you may place a figurine behind each bowl—the crone figure behind the bowl on the left, the pregnant figure behind the center bowl, and the baby or child figure behind the bowl on the right. In the small dish, pour a bit of honey. Dip your finger in and taste it, then offer the honey to the Goddess:

> "Eleithyia, midwife to goddesses and women, I taste the sweetness of Your presence and offer You golden honey in thanks for Your aid. Grant me a vision today, that I may see the face of the child who will soon be born from my belly."

Close your eyes, quiet your mind, and concentrate on the taste of the honey on your tongue. Slowly open your

Ancient Spellcraft

eyes and gaze into the bowl on the left. Allow your focus to get fuzzy. Scrying works best when you don't try too hard—just let the images come as they may. When you feel it is time, shift your gaze to the center bowl, and finally to the bowl on the right. When you have seen all there is to see, thank the Goddess:

"Eleithyia, I thank You for the sweet visions You have granted me. May You ever keep watch over the growing bellies of womankind."

Take the honey outside and give it to the Earth, who is the body of the Goddess. Empty the bowls of water into the ground as well, thinking all the while of the wonders you have seen.

The Apple of Your Eye

The ancient Celts celebrated a feast of the dead at the end of their harvest season, a time we now refer to as Samhain or Halloween. Apples played a special role at this time of the year. They represented immortality as the fruit of the Crone-Goddess Morrigu who ruled the land of death (Tir na nOg) in the West. Slice an apple in half horizontally and you will see a pentagram of seeds, the Goddess' promise of immortality in Her land of the dead over the western horizon. As a symbol of immortality, the apple represents the soul, that part of us that makes us each who we are. Pigs that were sacrificed to the Celtic Crone-Goddess were roasted with an apple in their mouth, symbolic of the soul that travels to the Land in the West. This is the origin of the medieval tradition of placing an apple in the mouth of a roasted boar.

Apples played such an important role in Samhain ceremonies that they have continued to play a role in modern Halloween festivities as well. Bobbing for apples is a game descended from these Samhain ceremonies, one that is still popular today. Their red color has long caused apples to be associated with love as well as with the Goddess. Since they are sacred to the Goddess, Who knows everything, apples can be used to tap into Her knowledge and learn who a future spouse might be. This divination is best performed at Samhain because at this time of year the veil between the worlds is thinnest, but it can be performed successfully at any time of year provided you avoid distractions and concentrate well as you fall asleep.

The Divination
What you will need:

- ✦ An apple, preferably a bright red one. Red represents the passion of the Goddess and the blood (especially menstrual blood) that creates life.
- ✦ A knife to cut the apple with. This should be a ritual knife, if you have one, or the best knife in your kitchen.

Ancient Spellcraft

- ✦ A clean white handkerchief.
- ✦ Pen and paper.

Performing the divination:

Late at night as you are getting ready to go to bed, clear your mind and quiet your surroundings. In order for the Goddess' visions to appear to you, you must have a clear and quiet mind as you go to sleep. Any expectations you harbor will cloud the vision and distract from it. Some people find that staring at a candle flame is a good way to clear the mind. When your mind is quiet and distracting thoughts have ceased, pick up the apple and look at it. It is a fruit, the beginning of new life. It is red, the color of passion and life's blood. It is round, the shape of the infinite, yet finite, circle.

Carefully cut the apple in half horizontally. Look at the cut surfaces. The seeds in the apple core create a five-fold pentagram pattern, an ancient symbol of the magick of life itself. Carefully pick out the seeds and lay them on the handkerchief. Put the apple halves back together and set the apple next to your bed. Fold the seeds in the handkerchief and place it under your pillow. Lie down to sleep, keeping your mind clear and quiet as you fall asleep. The Goddess will offer you visions and dreams about your future life and loves. When you wake up in the morning, before you get out of bed, write down all you remember of your dreams before the memories fade. Now you have a record of your visions to compare to future events.

The game of life brings with it a powerful element of chance, the intertwining of the free will of many individuals moving along their life paths. We simple humans cannot see into the future, cannot know what will happen beyond the weatherman's five-day forecast. So we turn to our deities, to the same powerful figures who have guided and aided humankind for age upon age. Call to them when you are lost, when you have come to a fork in the road, when your intuition asks you to listen a little more closely to a higher voice. They will aid you in your quest, just as they have aided so many people for so many millennia.

BIBLIOGRAPHY

Biers, William R. *Archaeology of Greece: An Introduction.* Ithaca, N.Y.: Cornell University Press, 1987.

Bulfinch, Thomas. *Bulfinch's Mythology: The Age of Fable.* Garden City, N.Y.: Doubleday and Company, Inc., 1968.

Campbell, Joseph. *The Hero with a Thousand Faces.* Bollinger Series. Princeton: Princeton University Press, 1973.

———. *The Masks of God.* Vols. I-IV. New York: Penguin Books, 1977.

———. *Myths to Live By.* New York: Penguin Books, 1972.

Castleden, Rodney. *The Knossos Labyrinth.* London: Routledge, 1990.

Clason, George S. *The Richest Man in Babylon.* New York: Signet Books, 1988.

Crawford, Harriet. *Sumer and the Sumerians.* Cambridge: Cambridge University Press, 1991.

d'Alviella, Count Goblet. *The Migration of Symbols.* New York: University Books, 1956.

de Selincourt, Aubrey. *The World of Herodotus.* Boston: Little, Brown and Company, 1962.

Dillon, Miles and Nora K. Chadwick. *The Celtic Realms.* New York: The New American Library, 1967.

Eliade, Mircea. *A History of Religious Ideas.* 3 vols. Chicago: The University of Chicago Press, 1985.

———. *Patterns in Comparative Religion.* Sheed and Ward, 1958.

Eliade, Mircea and Ioan P. Couliano. *The Eliade Guide to World Religions.* San Francisco: HarperSanFrancisco, 1991.

Ellis, Peter Beresford. *The Chronicles of the Celts: New tellings of their myths and legends.* New York: Carroll and Graf Publishers, Inc., 1999.

Frazer, Sir James George. *The Golden Bough: A Study in Magic and Religion.* Abridged edition. New York: The Macmillan Company, 1951.

Gimbutas, Marija. *The Goddesses and Gods of Old Europe: Myths and Cult Images.* Berkeley: University of California Press, 1974.

Graves, Robert. *The White Goddess: A historical grammar of poetic myth.* Farrar Straus and Cudahy, Inc., 1948.

Grimal, Pierre. *The Dictionary of Classical Mythology.* Trans. A.R. Maxwell-Hyslop. London: Basil Blackwell Publisher Ltd., 1985.

Hamilton, Edith. *Mythology.* Boston: Little, Brown and Co., 1969.

Herm, Gerhard. *The Phoenicians: The Purple Empire of the Ancient World.* Trans. Caroline Hillier. New York: William Morrow and Company, Inc., 1975.

Higgins, Reynold. *The Archaeology of Minoan Crete.* New York: Henry Z. Walck, Inc., 1973.

Leach, Maria, ed. *Standard Dictionary of Folklore, Mythology, and Legend.* New York: Funk & Wagnalls Co., 1950.

Bibliography

MacQueen, J. G. *The Hittites and their Contemporaries in Asia Minor.* Boulder, Colo.: Westview Press, 1975.

Mallory, J. P. *In Search of the Indo-Europeans: Language, Archaeology and Myth.* London: Thames and Hudson, 1989.

Marinatos, Nanno. *Minoan Religion: Ritual, Image and Symbol.* Columbia, South Carolina: University of South Carolina Press, 1993.

Massa, Aldo. *The Phoenicians.* Trans. David Macrae. Geneva: Editions Minerva, 1977.

Monaghan, Patricia. *Book of Goddesses and Heroines.* New York: Dutton, 1981.

Nilsson, M.P. *Minoan-Mycenaean Religion.* Cambridge University Press, 1950.

_____. *The Mycenaean Origin of Greek Mythology.* Cambridge University Press, 1932.

Oates, Joan. *Babylon.* Revised edition. New York: Thames and Hudson, 1986.

Pallotino, Massimo. *The Etruscans.* Trans. J. Cremona. Bloomington, Ind.: Indiana University Press, 1975.

Panati, Charles. *Sacred Origins of Profound Things: The stories behind the rites and rituals of the world's religions.* New York: Penguin Books, 1996.

Pennick, Nigel. *Magical Alphabets.* York Beach, Maine: Samuel Weiser, Inc., 1992.

Piggott, Stuart. *The Druids.* New York: Praeger Publishers, Inc., 1975.

Raftery, Barry. *Pagan Celtic Ireland: The Enigma of the Irish Iron Age.* New York: Thames and Hudson, 1994.

Saggs, H. W. F. *Everyday Life in Babylonia and Assyria.* New York: Dorset Press, 1965.

Stone, Merlin. *When God Was a Woman.* New York: Barnes and Noble, Inc., 1976.

Vandenberg, Philipp. *The Mystery of the Oracles.* New York: Macmillan Publishing Co., Inc.

Walker, Barbara. *The Woman's Encyclopedia of Myths and Secrets.* San Francisco: HarperCollins, 1983.

Warren, Peter. *The Aegean Civilizations.* New York: Peter Bedrick Books, 1989.

Watkins, Calvert, ed. *The American Heritage Dictionary of Indo-European Roots.* Boston: Houghton Mifflin Company, 1985.

Webster's New Collegiate Dictionary. Springfield, MA: G & C Merriam Co., 1979.

Wolkstein, Diane and Samuel Noah Kramer. *Inanna, Queen of Heaven and Earth.* New York: Harper and Row Publishers, 1983.

Wood, Michael. *Legacy: The Search for Ancient Cultures.* New York: Sterling Publishing Company, Inc., 1992.

Index

A

Acropolis, 48
Actaeon, 127
Admete, 150
Aengus, 43
Aetna, 141-143
Alcohol, and spells, 31-32
Allah, 43
Amalthea, 154
Amun-Ra, 46
Ananke, 45
Ancient civilization,
    and culture, 37-40
    and religious history, 21-24
Ancient Empires, map of, 40
Ankh, 93-95
Apalunas, 148-150
Aphrodite, 48, 87-89
Apollo, 47, 48, 51, 139-141, 152, 198
Apples, 91-93, 210-212
Ariadne, 45, 75-78, 95-98, 113-115, 183-185
Artemis, 127

Asclepius, 177-180
Astarte, 42, 51
Athena, 48, 143-145

B

Baal, 42, 51
Babylonians, 10
    history of, 41-42
Birch tree, 70-72
Birds, 68-70
Blackthorn shrub, 166
Brigid, 43, 163-164
Brooms, 67-68, 160-161
Byblos, 42

C

Canaanites, 10,
    history of, 38, 42-43
Cardea, 164-166
Carmenta, 18
Celts, 9, 10
    and divinations, 201, 210-211
    and fertility spells, 127-129

and healing, 180-182, 186-187, 191
and prosperity spells, 70-72
and protection spells, 162-164
history of, 43-44
Centaurs, 180-182
Cernunnos, 43
Cherries, 98-99
Chiron, 180-182
Clothing, 115-116, 191-192
Cooling spells, 188-189
Cornucopia, 63-64
Crane Dance, 95-96
Cretans, 9-10
   and divination, 208
   and healing spells, 175-177, 182-185
   and prosperity spells, 56-60, 64-66, 68-70, 75-78
   and protection spells, 145-147, 154-156, 159-160
   and romance spells, 95-98, 113-115, 122-125, 127-129
   history of, 44-45
Crocus, 75-76
Cronos, 45, 56
Cupid, 89-90
Cybele, 110-113

D

Daphne, 98
Deities, 21-24
   and civilization, 37-40
   and respect, 24-26
Delphi, 139, 198-199
Demeter, 60-63, 67-68, 141
Disposal, and spells, 25-26

Divinations,
   for future children, 208-210
   for future spouse, 211-212
   with dominoes, 206-208
   with laurel leaves and incense, 199-201
   with lightening, 203-205
   with stones, 202-203
Dogs, 149-150, 186-187
Dragon's blood, 113-115
Druids, 201-202
   and calendar, 70

E

Ea, 42, 49
Eagles, 137-138
Egypt, 9, 10
   and fertility spells, 129-130
   and romance spells, 93-95, 100-102
   history of, 45-46
Eleithyia, 45, 159-160, 208-210
Elements of ritual, 27
Elephants, 117-118
Enki, 52, 73-75
Ereshkigal, 49, 52
Etruscans, 10
   and divination, 203-205
   and romance spells, 90-93
   history of, 46-47
Europa, 65-66

F

Fate, goddess of, 45
Father Time, 45, 57
Fish, 73-75
Footprints, 147
Fortuna, 63-64

Index

G
Ge, 141
Gilgamesh, 52
Gorgon, 144-145
Grain, 60-62, 67
Great Mother Goddess, 144
Great Mother Ocean, 45
Greeks, 29,
   and healing spells, 189-190
   and prosperity spells, 60-62, 67-68
   and protection spells, 137-138, 139-141, 143-145, 150-151, 152-153, 160-162
   and romance spells, 87-89, 98-100, 102-104
   history of, 48
Griffin, 145-147
Grim Reaper, 57

H
Halloween, 210
Hannahanna, 49
Harvest, 56-57
Hathor, 46, 117
Hatti, 125-127
Healing, 10
   defined, 171
Hecate, 120, 160-162
Hephaestos, 141
Hera, 48, 150-151
Hermaphrodite, 87
Hermes, 87-89, 152-153
Hieros gamos, 103-104
Hippocampus, 78-80
Hittities, 10
   and divination, 206-208
   and fertility spells, 125-127
   and protection spells, 148-150
   history of, 48-49
Honey, 159-160, 209-210
Horned gods, and Celts, 43
Hwt-Hrw, 46
Hygeia, 189-190

I
Inanna, 42, 52
Indic priests, 28
Isis, 46, 117

J
Janus, 164-165
Juno, 47, 51, 115-116
Jupiter, 47, 51

K
Karma, 19, 25
Kumarbi, 49

L
Labrynth, 95-97
Labrys, 182-185
Life cycle, 56-57
Lightening, 203-205
Lily, 113-115
Lions, 110-111
Lottery, 206
Luis, 162-163

M
Maat, 46
Marduk, 24-25, 41
Mari, 102-103
Mars, 47, 51
Mecca, 42, 43

Medusa, 144-145
Menat, 101-102
Mercury, 89
Meri-Ra, 100
Min, 129-131
Minelathos, 127-129
Minoans, 44
Minocapros, 127
Minotauros, 122
Mohammed, 43
Moon-Bull, 44-45, 122-125
Moon-Stag, 127
Morrigu, 43, 210
Mother Ocean, 122-125
Mother Time, 57
Muses, 139

N

Neptune, 102
Nergal, 52
Ninlil, 49
Nut, 46

O

Ogham, 162-163, 166
Oracles, 198-199
Ouroboros, 87

P

Palm trees, 129-130
Parchment, and spells, 32
Phoenician purple, 50
Phoenicians, 10
   and prosperity spells, 78-81
   history of, 49-51
Poseidon, 48, 102
Pray, history of, 24
Prosperity, 10, 55

Protection, defined, 135
Pythia, 199-200
Repetition, and spells, 28-29
Rhea, 45, 56-60, 154-156, 175-177
Ritual, elements of, 27
Romance, 10, 85
Romans, 18
   and fertility spells, 115-116,
   and healing spells,185-186, 191-193
   and prosperity spells, 63-64,
   and protection spells, 156-159, 164-166,
   and romance spells, 89-90, 102-104
   history of, 51

S

Sacrifice, 26-27
   god of, 45
Saffron, 75-76
Samhain, 210-211
Season cycles,
   and Babylonians, 41
   and Celts, 43
Seawater, 122-124
Spells,
   and alcohol, 31-32
   and disposal, 25-26
   and repetition, 28-29
   and safety, 24-26
   and space, 29-31
   etymology of, 17-18
   for abundance, 65-66
   for agricultural fertility, 121-122, 123-125

Index

for bringing desire, 103-104
for bringing joy, 101-102
for bringing love, 87-89, 90, 91-93, 94-95, 96-98, 99-100, 101-102
for changing bad luck, 67-68, 71-72
for chronic illness, 173-175, 189-190, 193-194
for compromise, 142-143
for detoxifying, 192-193
for good fortune, 63-64
for healing, 176-177, 178-180, 180-182, 191
for home protection, 138, 149-150
for honesty, 139-141
for human fertility, 109-110, 111-113, 113-115, 116, 118-119
for life transformation, 183-185
for male virility, 126-127, 128-129, 130-131
for prosperous harvest, 58-60, 61-62
for protection against theft, 151, 152-153
for protection during childbirth, 159-160
for protection from the supernatural, 163-164, 165-166, 167-168
for protection of babies and children, 155-156, 157-159, 161-162
for protection of life, 146-147, 148
for protection of women, 144-145
for removing illness, 185-186, 186-187
for removing negativity, 69-70
for success in business, 74-75, 75-78, 79-81
purpose of, 19-20
Straif, 166
Sumerians, 10
    and fertility spells, 120
    and prosperity spells, 73-75,
    history of, 51-52
Sun gods,
    and Egyptians, 46
    and Hittites, 49
Sybil, 199

T

Tin, 47, 203-205
Turan, 47, 90-93

U

Ur, 172-175
Uranus, 141

V

Venus, 47, 51, 89
Vesta, 156-159
Votum, 27-28, 64

W

Wildlife gods, and Celts, 43
Wurusemu, 49, 108-110

Z

Zagreus, 45, 154, 175

About the Author

Laura Perry lives in the Atlanta, Georgia area with her husband and daughter. She has been fascinated with the ancient world since high school and has studied the history and spirituality of ancient cultures as a hobby for many years. A professional holistic health consultant with a Master's degree in Natural Health, Laura is currently working to earn a Doctorate in Naturopathy. Laura feels this career choice meshes well with her interest in Earth-oriented spirituality, focusing on healthy living (both physical and spiritual) and respect for all life forms.

Laura is a teacher and priestess in the local pagan community. She was the founder and editor of *Hephaestos' Forge*, the newsletter for disabled pagans, throughout its four-year existence. She is currently the Atlanta Area Coordinator for the Goddess 2000 Project, which brings goddess spirituality to life for people of all paths through music, dance, and hands-on creative art projects.

Laura studied Mayan mythology and spiritual practices, both ancient and modern, and has traveled to Central America to further her studies. She has also traveled across the American Southeast, Southwest, and Eastern seaboard pursuing her interest in Native American cultures.